COURAGEOUS FAITH

Through the Year

Bill Hybels

Compiled and edited by Keri Wyatt Kent

InterVarsity Press
Downers Grove, Illinois
Leicester, England

InterVarsity Press, USA
P.O. Box 1400, Downers Grove, IL 60515-1426, USA
World Wide Web: www.ivpress.com
E-mail: mail@ivpress.com

Inter-Varsity Press, England
38 De Montfort Street, Leicester LE1 7GP, England
World Wide Web: www.ivpbooks.com
E-mail: ivp@uccf.org.uk

InterVarsity Press®, U.S.A., is the book-publishing division of InterVarsity Christian Fellowship/USA® <www.intervarsity.org>.

Inter-Varsity Press, England, is the book-publishing division of the Universities and Colleges Christian Fellowship (formerly the Inter-Varsity Fellowship), a student movement linking Christian Unions in universities and colleges throughout the United Kingdom and the Republic of Ireland, and a member movement of the International Fellowship of Evangelical Students. For information about local and national activities write to UCCF, 38 De Montfort Street, Leicester LE1 7GP.

Design: Cindy Kiple
Images: Johner/Photonica
USA ISBN 0-8308-3294-7
UK ISBN 1-84474-041-2
Printed in the United States of America ∞

Library of Congress Cataloging-in-Publication Data

Hybels, Bill.
  Courageous faith through the year / Bill Hybels; compiled and
  edited by Keri Wyatt Kent.
    p. cm.
  "The devotions are adapted from several books by Bill Hybels: Too
busy not to pray, Making life work and Who you are when no one's
looking, as well as the booklet Finding God in the storms of
life"—Introd. ISBN 0-8308-3294-7 (pbk.: alk. paper)
  1. Devotional calendars. I. Kent, Keri Wyatt, 1963- II. Title
BV4811.H93 2004
242'.2—dc22

                                                                          2004004606

British Library Cataloguing in Publication Data
A catalogue record for this book is available from the British Library.

| **P** | 18 | 17 | 16 | 15 | 14 | 13 | 12 | 11 | 10 | 9 | 8 | 7 | 6 | 5 | 4 | 3 | 2 | 1 |
| **Y** | 18 | 17 | 16 | 15 | 14 | 13 | 12 | 11 | 10 | 09 | 08 | 07 | 06 | 05 | 04 | | | |

God's Work in You

Unless the LORD builds the house, its builders labor in vain.

PSALM 127:1

As you use this book, you will learn about prayer, about character, about building a courageous faith. I'll often suggest ideas for you to think about, pray about, or to do. A word of caution, however. This is not a book about how to get God to sit up and notice you or how to improve your heavenly credit rating. Prayer, wisdom and strength of character are important, but none of them is a way to earn salvation. That is because salvation cannot be earned—not even by courage, discipline, vision, endurance and love. The principles in this book will help you to grow, but only after you have accepted God's gift of life in him.

At the bottom of each page is an activity that gives you a place to start in responding to the Scripture and accompanying thoughts. That activity may be to reflect, to pray or to meditate. Responding to what God has said to you in the daily meditation is always important. Simply reading something will have little effect on you. The suggestion is just a place to start, however, and you may find yourself praying about what you reflected on, and times of meditation should usually end in prayer too.

Beyond that, you may feel led to journal. Especially if the reflection raises confusion within you, it can be helpful to write your thoughts down on paper. Also, some prayers are better written in a journal because you need to be as concrete as possible in your ideas. And sometimes God will speak to you through reflection and meditation in a way that's so downright stunning that these thoughts should be recorded and read for several days.

You'll find a year's worth of devotions here, designed to fill six days a week. We choose to offer six rather than seven for a built-in bit of grace as circumstances do sometimes infringe on our devotional time. But you can use the seventh day to go back to some of the "pray," "journal" and "apply" suggestions you'll find at the end of the devotion.

These devotions are not dated; you can start anywhere and move around as you please. There are devotions appropriate for Holy Week and the Easter season in weeks 15 and 16. If you want devotions appropriate for Christmas, you may enjoy the reflections on rest in week 51 as an antidote to holiday stress.

The devotions are adapted from several books by Bill Hybels: *Too Busy Not to Pray, Making Life Work* and *Who You Are When No One's Looking,* as well as the booklet *Finding God in the Storms of Life.* If you want to read more on these themes, you may want to look for those books.

As you begin your journey through the year, talk to God about your motives for reading this book. Thank him that you don't have to earn his approval. Tell him about your desire to grow, and thank him for promising to meet you.

Winter

M O N D A Y *Saved by Grace*

For it is by grace you have been saved, through faith—
and this not from yourselves, it is the gift of God—
not by works, so that no one can boast.

EPHESIANS 2:8

Salvation is a gift from the heavenly Father to us. It cost him everything—the death of his beloved only Son. It costs us nothing. Hard work cannot earn it; neither can good behavior or sterling character. The only way we can enjoy a relationship with God is by coming to Jesus Christ, our hands outstretched and empty, and saying, "Lord, I want to follow you. Please take me into your family, scrub me, give me new clothes and make me like you." And Jesus will do exactly that. He will take us as we are and assure us that we are his forever. Then—slowly at first, but surely—he will mold us and shape us until we resemble him.

APPLY: *Are you confident that you have a relationship with God through the grace of Jesus Christ? If so, thank him for loving you enough to accept you in spite of your sin. If you have never accepted Christ, decide now to do whatever it takes to earnestly seek him and come into relationship with him.*

TUESDAY

Living in God's Presence

I am the vine, you are the branches.
Those who abide in me and I in them bear much fruit,
because apart from me you can do nothing.

JOHN 15:5 NRSV

How can we abide in Christ, and bear spiritual fruit? Reading God's Word and spending time in prayer are good first steps. Prayer is a way to maintain constant communion with God the Father and God the Son through God the Holy Spirit. It is the means of living out the intense relationship Jesus described.

We're called to abide in him, but God also promises that he will abide in us! Awareness of God's presence comes as the result of taking time to speak and listen to him. When you practice being aware of God's presence, you pick up his signals all throughout the day. At work, at home, in your car or wherever you are, you begin to dialogue with the Lord. It has nothing to do with being in a church building or on your knees. It has to do with God's presence in and around you—"Christ in you, the hope of glory" (Colossians 1:27).

APPLY: *Do you experience the presence of God in your daily life? Promise yourself that you will use this book to more deeply abide in God's presence.*

A Glimpse of God's Plan

> Moses said to the LORD, "O Lord, I have never been eloquent. . . .
> I am slow of speech and tongue."
> The LORD said to him, "Who gave man his mouth?
> Who makes him deaf or mute? Who gives him sight or makes him blind?
> Is it not I, the LORD? Now go; I will help you speak and will teach you what to say."

EXODUS 4:10-12

Vision is the God-given ability to catch a glimpse of what God wants to do through your life if you dedicate yourself to him.

In the story above, Moses had no vision of how God could use him. I have to admit that I share Moses' problem. My life is not earmarked for greatness. There is no aura of drama about it. I feel plenty ordinary most of the time, and I often wonder if I matter at all.

But every once in a while when I'm in tune with the Lord, the Holy Spirit seems to whisper to me, "Hybels, take your blinders off. Where's your vision? You're not much, but God is. And you matter to him. Why don't you believe what you preach?" God's challenges to me give me the courage to keep following him.

PRAY: *Pray a listening prayer. What is God whispering to you about his plan for your life? Let go of the objections that fear or lack of vision cause you to raise.*

Bars or Stars?

Where there is no vision, the people perish.

PROVERBS 29:18 KJV

The story is told of two prisoners in one small cell with no light except what came through a tiny window three feet above eye level. Both prisoners spent a great deal of time looking at that window, of course. One of them saw the bars—obvious, ugly, metallic reminders of reality. From day to day he grew increasingly discouraged, bitter, angry and hopeless. By contrast, the other prisoner looked through the window to the stars beyond. Hope welled up in that prisoner as he began to think of the possibility of starting a new life in freedom.

The prisoners were looking at the same window, but one saw bars while the other saw stars. And the difference in their vision made a huge difference in their lives. Likewise, our vision will affect our whole life.

APPLY: *Are you focusing on the bars in your life, or looking to the stars? Do you have a vision for what God wants to do in your life? Have you considered that you and the people around you will be given life through your vision?*

Simon and his brother Andrew [were] casting a net into the lake,
for they were fishermen. "Come, follow me," Jesus said, "and I will make you fishers of men."
At once they left their nets and followed him.

MARK 1:16-18

At some time in your life you must have sensed God saying to you, "It's time to start going in a new direction. I want you to change vocations (go back to school, start a ministry, strike up a friendship, get a job, go to the mission field), because you matter to me. I have great plans for you, and I'm going to work in your life. If you'll just take those blinders off, I'll use you." Just for a moment you felt a flutter in your heart, and you thought, "Maybe that was God's voice." But then instead of looking at stars, you focused on bars.

I cannot ask you to do something that I am not willing to do. I want to be more willing to say, "God, here I am. Use me. Lead me. If you have something significant planned for my life, count me in. I'll follow you the best I know how—trembling, but trusting. I want to see stars, not bars. I want to grow in vision."

APPLY: *Do you sense God leading you in a new direction? Are you willing to grow in vision and follow him?*

Working Toward Vision

> *My eyes are ever on the LORD, for only he will release my feet from the snare.*
>
> PSALM 25:15

Vision is on my endangered character quality list, along with courage and discipline. The reason is simple: it takes too much work to be a visionary. It's much easier just to go with the flow and do what's expected. It takes courage to break out of conventional thought patterns. It takes confidence and daring to risk failure with a new idea or a new approach. Visionaries tend to fail many times before they ever succeed, and most people would rather be safe and secure.

It also takes a lot of old-fashioned perspiration to be a visionary. It takes discipline to sit down with a pencil and paper and vow not to get up from your desk until you come up with five new ways to do something. It takes endurance to get on your knees and stay there until God supernaturally ignites a fresh thought in your mind. It takes hard work to plan for what could happen in five years in your business, family, marriage or ministry. But developing vision deepens and strengthens our faith.

APPLY: *What prevents you from keeping your eyes on God and following him? Where do you need a new, visionary approach? Ask God for a vision and the courage to carry it out.*

MONDAY

Radical Love

> *Jesus replied: "'Love the Lord your God with all your heart*
> *and with all your soul and with all your mind.'*
> *This is the first and greatest commandment.*
> *And the second is like it: 'Love your neighbor as yourself.'"*

MATTHEW 22:37-39

As Jesus clearly taught, the highest priority in the life of every believer should be to love God. Our second-highest priority should be to love people, all of whom matter to God, in a radical, nonretaliatory, second-mile way.

For two thousand years people have read and reread Jesus' Sermon on the Mount, asking the Spirit of God to help them understand and apply its wisdom. Believers have drawn a wide range of conclusions, and I still have a lot of questions about its implications myself. But these stories have some general applications that are as plain as can be. There's no mystery about them.

One obvious principle is that retaliation is a dead-end road. Revenge only perpetrates and escalates animosity. Somebody has to stop the senseless escalation—and God wants that someone to be you and me.

JOURNAL: *Write about your reaction to Jesus' three illustrations of radical love in Matthew 5:38-42. What do you think God is calling you to do? What barriers stand in your way of loving people in a radical, nonretaliatory way?*

Breaking the Hostility Cycle

You have heard that it was said, "Eye for eye, and tooth for tooth."
But I tell you, Do not resist an evil person.
If someone strikes you on the right cheek, turn to him the other also.

MATTHEW 5:38-39

I think that when Jesus preached these now-familiar words, he was trying to startle his disciples into taking the next step in their understanding of Christian love.

Can you imagine how hard it must have been for the disciples to hear Jesus' challenge? Born and raised in a revenge-oriented culture, they knew all about male honor, bravado and machismo. Turn the other cheek? A crazy idea like that shakes us from our complacency.

Even as your enemy slaps you, God is trying to reach out to him. In fact, he is looking for someone through whom he could love this guy. So dig down deep into the foundations of your faith and love him. Do something radical that will mark his life. If turning the other cheek to him for a second slap will make a mark on the man's soul, turn the other cheek.

APPLY: *Who do you have a difficult time loving—someone who insults or cuts you down? What would it look like for you to "turn the other cheek" in your relationship?*

But I tell you who hear me: Love your enemies, do good to those who hate you,
bless those who curse you, pray for those who mistreat you.
If someone strikes you on one cheek, turn to him the other also.

LUKE 6:27-29

In the culture of first-century Jerusalem, receiving a slap in the face was considered the ultimate degradation. Even today when we are insulted, we say, "That was a real slap in the face." There's no doubt about it—you have been publicly humiliated by an arrogant, opinionated ignoramus. You can still feel the sting of his slap on your face. Your adrenaline is flowing; your anger level is skyrocketing. Your honor is at stake. You know you could knock this guy into the middle of next week if you wanted to. And inside your head, voices are saying, "Rocky, Rocky, Rocky . . ."

The moment of truth has arrived. What are you going to do? In the Sermon on the Mount, Jesus commands his followers to show radical love. Don't slap him back. Don't scream at him. Don't kick him in the shins. Don't curse him under your breath. Instead, look the man straight in the eye and remind yourself that, in spite of his arrogance and anger, he matters to God.

PRAY: *Bless those who curse you; pray for those who mistreat you.*

THURSDAY

An Amazing Command

If someone wants to sue you and take your tunic,
let him have your cloak as well.

MATTHEW 5:40

In New Testament times, people wore an inner garment and a heavy, warm outer garment that served as a coat during the day and a blanket at night.

In that climate a man without an outer garment for warmth at night was in a bad way. It was common for men to hold each other's garments as collateral in trading deals until the goods were delivered. Usually the inner garment was demanded, because most people would have an extra one. Ordinarily the outer garment was not used, because it was illegal to keep another man's outer garment overnight, even if the man reneged on his part of the deal. The cloak had to be returned at sunset, because without it he would have nothing to protect him from the night's chill.

In view of this, Jesus' command is amazing. If you are making a deal with someone and can't come through with your end of it, and if that man demands an inner garment as overnight collateral, give it to him. But go a step further. Offer him your outer garment as well. That's sacrificial love.

APPLY: *How would keeping your end of a bargain in business, even when it causes you discomfort or inconvenience, help you to build a courageous faith?*

The Second Mile

If someone forces you to go one mile, go with him two miles. . . .
Love your enemies and pray for those who persecute you.

MATTHEW 5:41-44

In those days, Israel was ruled by Rome. A Roman soldier had the legal right to approach any civilian at any time of the day or night and impress—that is, coerce—him into service.

The Jews particularly hated it when a Roman soldier made them carry baggage. Whenever troop assignments were shifted, soldiers would appear, tap Jewish men on the shoulder with spears, and say, "Carry that suitcase." No matter what the civilian was doing—sleeping, plowing a field, selling his wares—he would have to quit and do as the soldier said. There was a limit, however. Roman soldiers could force a Jewish man to carry baggage for no more than a mile at a time.

So suppose a Roman soldier grabs you by the scruff of the neck, hands you a heavy duffle and says, "Carry this, pal." How does Jesus say to respond? When you get to the end of the obligatory mile, instead of slamming the suitcase to the ground hoping to break something fragile inside, instead of spitting on the ground to show your contempt for this pagan soldier, show him radical love.

PRAY: *What second mile is God asking you to go? Listen to God's direction on this question.*

The Power of Love

A new command I give you: Love one another.
As I have loved you, so you must love one another.
By this all men will know that you are my disciples, if you love one another.

JOHN 13:34-35

God challenges us to become radical, nonretaliatory, second-mile lovers because nothing leaves a deeper mark on the lives of spiritually hardened men and women than seeing radical love in action.

If you know the love of Jesus Christ in a personal way, you may sometimes lie awake nights thinking of ways to make a mark on people's lives so that they too will come to enjoy what you have found. Should you wear a little lapel pin? Put a bumper sticker on your car? Display a large Bible in your office? Tell people that you don't go to movies or buy sexually explicit rock albums?

Jesus says, if you really want to make a deep, lasting mark on someone, demonstrate radical love. There is so much compelling power in that kind of love that it makes callous people's heads spin. They cannot figure out why you are giving up your rights and letting someone take advantage of you. But that kind of radical love gets people asking questions—questions that often lead them to God.

PRAY: *Ask God to give you the power to love others in a radically unselfish way.*

M O N D A Y *Distorted Vision*

> *When he had spit on the [blind] man's eyes and put his hands on him,*
> *Jesus asked, "Do you see anything?"*
> *He looked up and said, "I see people; they look like trees walking around."*
> *Once more Jesus put his hands on the man's eyes.*
> *Then his eyes were opened, his sight was restored, and he saw everything clearly.*

MARK 8:23-25

Shortly after becoming a Christian, I realized I needed a lot of softening. I needed help in becoming kind, gentle and tenderhearted toward others.

One day I read the passage above. I feasted on the words, "I see men; but they look like trees, walking." I thought, "That's my problem too. I don't see men very clearly. People, as far as I'm concerned, are just part of the landscape. When I look around and see other people, I don't think, 'Wow, this person is a custom-designed creation of the almighty God. He has God's image stamped on him. He is the object of God's greatest affection. Jesus shed his blood for him.' I don't think like that. For me, people are like trees, walking." And when I realized how far my view of people was from Jesus' view, I knew I needed my vision changed.

JOURNAL: *Write about your current view of people and how God might want to change it.*

Extraordinary Treasures

Are not two sparrows sold for a penny?
Yet not one of them will fall to the ground apart from the will of your Father.
And even the very hairs of your head are all numbered.
So don't be afraid; you are worth more than many sparrows.

MATTHEW 10:29-31

Hardhearted people tend to divide the world into winners and losers, heavyweights and lightweights, survivors and basket cases, sharp and two bricks short of a load. It is hard for them to realize that they have never bumped into just an ordinary person—that every living, walking, breathing human being is an extraordinary treasure in God's eyes. It is hard for them to grasp that losers and basket cases matter to God every bit as much as winners and survivors; that Russians, Cubans, Libyans and Palestinians are just as important to God as Americans; that God loves prisoners, homosexuals and bag ladies as much as he loves stock brokers, dental students and seminarians. Everyone matters to God. Often, hardhearted people can begin to see this only when God begins to soften their heart.

PRAY: *Thank God that he values each and every human being on the planet, including you. Pray for the people you might think of as "losers," and ask God to bless them. Ask him to help you see the value of each person, no matter what.*

WEDNESDAY *Accept Others*

*Accept one another, then, just as Christ has accepted you,
in order to bring praise to God.*

ROMANS 15:7

All human beings are God's beloved creations, and all are invited to receive forgiveness at the cross. Because God has invited everybody into his family through Christ, every person we meet is a potential brother or sister. When we grasp this truth and begin to see people for what they mean to God, we begin to soften up and treat people tenderly.

The next time you're rude to someone because he or she is only a waitress, only a parking lot attendant, only the butcher or baker or candlestick maker—stop! There are no "only's" in God's eyes. These people may be doing humble work, but each one is extraordinary to God. Each one matters. Employers, if you have to give an employee a pink slip, don't just "sack" her. Remember that she matters to God. Single people, if you feel you should break up with the person you are dating, don't just "dump" him. Remember that he matters to God. Drivers, next time someone shakes his fist at you in traffic, don't snarl back. Remember that even hotheads matter to God. And God's treasures should be treated tenderly.

APPLY: *What does it mean to accept people the way that Christ accepted you? What might you need to change about your attitudes toward others?*

Other People's Shoes

Surely he took up our infirmities and carried our sorrows.

ISAIAH 53:4

I remember years ago going with Lynne to see *Sophie's Choice,* a psychological drama set in a World War II extermination camp. The movie was intense. Holding her two children in her arms, Sophie had to decide which one to hand over to the Nazis for sure incineration.

"This is pretty heavy drama," I thought. "But it's getting a bit long. I wonder if the popcorn stand is still open?" As I turned to look, I noticed that Lynne was sobbing. I decided to get popcorn another time.

I did not know what was wrong until two days later when she finally told me, "I was picturing having Todd in one arm and Shauna in the other, and having thirty seconds to choose which one was going to live and which one was going to die. How in the world would I ever make that choice?" Lynne had not only put on Sophie's moccasins; she had crawled into her socks, her dress and her bonnet.

This did not happen to me. I stayed outside the characters' skins and simply observed. Empathy does not always come naturally, but thankfully, it can be developed.

A P P L Y : *Are you hardhearted or tenderhearted? If you're not sure, rent a movie like* Sophie's Choice. *Do you empathize with the characters, or stay outside of their shoes?*

Treat Others Like Jesus Would

In everything, do to others what you would have them do to you,
for this sums up the Law and the Prophets.

MATTHEW 7:12

It's vital to start seeing people as God's treasures. It's important to learn to empathize with them. But how should these feelings be expressed? Should I slobber all over people? Should I sell my house and join the Peace Corps? What does a tenderhearted Christian do?

Treat people the way Jesus Christ treats you, and the way you'd like to be treated. When you pray, the Lord listens attentively to every word you say. Why not treat your spouse, your children, your friends and your coworkers the same way? Slow down, turn off the television, close out any distractions and say, "I'm going to listen, because I really want to hear what you have to say."

When you make a mistake, Jesus lifts you up, forgives you, and continues to treat you with love and respect. Why not do the same for the people with whom you live, work and worship? When you feel lonely and insecure, the Holy Spirit stays by your side and assures you of God's love. Why not comfort the people you love when they are going through difficult times?

JOURNAL: *Write about how you would ideally like people to respond to you in various circumstances. Keep that list in mind when you're dealing with other people.*

Express Affection

You are precious in my sight, and honored, and I love you.

ISAIAH 43:4 NRSV

I have called you friends.

JOHN 15:15

No believer ever has to doubt God's affection. If God does not want his children wondering whether or not they are loved, why not express your own affection regularly so that your family, friends and coworkers know how you feel about them?

What will happen if we begin to see people as they are in God's eyes, walk in their shoes and treat them the way Christ treats us? The results will be unbelievable. After their initial shock, our spouses and children will go wild with joy. Our coworkers will shake their heads and say, "The whole atmosphere around here has changed—I wonder what has happened to old Harry Hardheart?" Our superficial friendships will deepen into warm brotherly or sisterly relationships. Our churches will multiply in effectiveness as people discover they can find love where Christ is worshiped.

PRAY: *Ask God to help you to treat others the way Christ has treated you. Start with your family, and ask God to show you how to empathize and be kind to them. Notice how praying for others changes the way you treat them.*

MONDAY *Grow in Prayer*

> *I sought the LORD, and he answered me; he delivered me from all my fears.*
> *Those who look to him are radiant; their faces are never covered with shame.*

PSALM 34:4-5

Prayer has not always been my strong suit. For many years, even as senior pastor of a large church, I knew more about prayer than I ever practiced in my own life. I have a racehorse temperament, and the tugs of self-sufficiency and self-reliance are very real to me.

God and I used to be rather casually related to one another. We didn't get together and talk very much. Now, however, we get together a lot, not talking on the run but carrying on substantial, soul-searching conversations every morning for a good chunk of time.

As you grow in prayer, God will reveal more of himself to you, breathing more of his life into your spirit. Mark my words, that will be the most fulfilling and rewarding part of your experience with prayer, more so even than the answers to prayer you are sure to receive. Fellowship with God, trust, confidence, peace, relief—these wonderful feelings will be yours as you learn how to pray.

JOURNAL: *Describe your current relationship with God. Is it as close and intimate as you desire? Journal about what changes you'd like to see in your relationship with him.*

A Channel for God's Power

What god is so great as our God? You are the God who performs miracles;
you display your power among the peoples.

PSALM 77:13-14

Why pray? People are drawn to prayer because they know that God's power flows primarily to people who pray.

The Scriptures overflow with passages teaching that our almighty, omnipotent God is ready, willing and able to answer the prayers of his followers. The miracles of Israel's exodus from Egypt and journey to the Promised Land were all answers to prayer. So were Jesus' miracles of stilling storms, providing food, healing the sick and raising the dead. As the early church grew, God answered the believers' continual prayers for healing and deliverance.

God's power can change circumstances and relationships. It can help us face life's daily struggles. It can heal psychological and physical problems, remove marriage obstructions, meet financial needs—in fact, it can handle any kind of difficulty, dilemma or discouragement.

Someone has said that when we work, *we* work; but when we pray, *God* works. His supernatural strength is available to praying people who are convinced that he can make a difference. Skeptics may argue that answered prayers are only coincidences, but as an English archbishop once observed, "It's amazing how many coincidences occur when one begins to pray."

PRAY: *Spend time this week asking God to work powerfully in a challenge you are currently facing.*

Moses said to Joshua . . . "Go out to fight the Amalekites.
Tomorrow I will stand on top of the hill with the staff of God in my hands."
So Joshua fought the Amalekites . . . and Moses, Aaron and Hur went to the top of the hill.
As long as Moses held up his hands, the Israelites were winning,
but whenever he lowered his hands, the Amalekites were winning.

EXODUS 17:9-11

Moses discovered that day that God's prevailing power is released through prayer. When I began praying in earnest, I discovered the same thing. It boils down to this: if you are willing to invite God to involve himself in your daily challenges, you will experience his prevailing power—in your home, in your relationships, in the marketplace, in the schools, in the church, wherever it is most needed.

That power may come in the form of wisdom—an idea you desperately need and can't come up with yourself. It may come in the form of courage greater than you could ever muster. It may come in the form of confidence or perseverance, uncommon staying power, a changed attitude toward a family member, changed circumstances, maybe even outright miracles. However it comes, God's prevailing power is released in the lives of people who pray.

JOURNAL: *Are you weary of praying? Write a prayer asking God for his strength and power in your life.*

Keep the Power Flowing

When Moses' hands grew tired, they took a stone and put it under him and he sat on it.
Aaron and Hur held his hands up—one on one side, one on the other—
so that his hands remained steady till sunset.
So Joshua overcame the Amalekite army with the sword.

EXODUS 17:12-13

Once Moses made the connection between prayer and God's power, he determined to spend the rest of the day praying for God's involvement in the battle. But his arms grew weary. He knew better than to drop them to his sides; he had done that and watched his troops get wiped out. So the two men who accompanied him up the hill found a stone he could sit on. Then each man crawled under an arm and helped Moses hold his arms up. What a picture—Moses being supported by caring people who wanted to help him keep the power flowing! Needless to say, Israel won the battle that day.

APPLY: *Identify one or two people who could "hold you up" and encourage you to keep praying. Make a phone call or an appointment to ask the person you identified to partner with you in encouraging one another to keep praying and to keep growing closer to God.*

Prevailing Power

> *Trust in the LORD with all your heart*
> *and lean not on your own understanding.*

PROVERBS 3:5

It is hard for God to release his power in your life when you put your hands in your pockets and say, "I can handle it on my own." If you do that, don't be surprised if one day you get the nagging feeling that the tide of battle has shifted against you and that you're fairly powerless to do anything about it.

Prayerless people cut themselves off from God's prevailing power, and the frequent result is the familiar feeling of being overwhelmed, overrun, beaten down, pushed around, defeated. Surprising numbers of people are willing to settle for lives like that. Don't be one of them. Nobody has to live like that. Prayer is the key to unlocking God's prevailing power in your life.

PRAY: *Spend some time praying about a specific situation where you want to unlock God's power in your life.*

A God Who Is Able

If any of you is lacking in wisdom, ask God
who gives to all generously and ungrudgingly, and it will be given to you.
But ask in faith, never doubting . . . for the doubter, being double-minded
and unstable in every way, must not expect to receive anything from the Lord.

JAMES 1:5-8 NRSV

Is God able? Is he omnipotent? If you don't own that doctrine, you might as well pitch prayer. If your prayers have clouds of doubt hanging over them, they won't get anywhere. Before getting down on your knees, review God's past acts of faithfulness and power in Scripture and in your own life. Tune your mind properly so that when you finally pray, it will be to a God who is able.

The more you are convinced of God's ability, the more he demonstrates his ability to you. Jesus says, "I tell you the truth, if anyone says to this mountain, 'Go, throw yourself into the sea,' and does not doubt in his heart but believes that what he says will happen, it will be done for him" (Mark 11:23). Believe that God will not only hear you, but answer!

PRAY: *Ask God to remove the clouds of doubt that get in the way of your prayers. Review your own personal history with God, and thank him for his past power and help.*

M O N D A Y

Praying for Peace

Do not be anxious about anything, but in everything, by prayer and petition,
with thanksgiving, present your requests to God.
And the peace of God, which transcends all understanding,
will guard your hearts and your minds in Christ Jesus.

PHILIPPIANS 4 : 6 - 7

Several years ago my father, a relatively young and active man, died of a heart attack. As I drove to my mother's house in Michigan, I wondered how I would continue to function without the person who believed in me more than anyone else ever has or ever will.

That night in bed, I wrestled with God. "Why did this happen? How can I put it all together in my mind and in my life? Am I going to recover from losing my father? If you really love me, how could you do this to me?"

Suddenly, in the middle of the night, everything changed. It was as if I had turned a corner and was now facing a new direction. God simply said, "I'm able. I'm enough for you. Right now you doubt this, but trust me." In the middle of the bleakest night I have ever known, one overpoweringly intimate moment with God gave me courage, reassurance and hope.

PRAY: *Have you ever wrestled with God? What anxieties or questions do you want to ask him right now? Spend some time talking with him about those things.*

Deep Needs

> *Now to him who is able to do immeasurably more than all we ask or imagine,*
> *according to his power that is at work within us,*
> *to him be glory in the church and in Christ Jesus.*

EPHESIANS 3:20-21

Most of us have to admit that we don't pray that often about our deepest needs. We get faint-hearted. We begin to pray, but we soon find our minds wandering, and we realize we're using empty phrases. We start to feel hypocritical, and soon we give up. It seems better to live with almost any difficult situation than to continue to pray ineffectively.

We reach out to God, because we know he is holding out loving arms toward us. But then we often fall back and try to face our difficulties in our own power, because at some basic and perhaps unconscious level we doubt if God really can make a difference in the problems we are facing.

It is well and good to believe that God loves us and wants to help us. The question remains: is he able to do so? Because if he isn't, all the good will in heaven and earth will make no difference.

PRAY: *What needs do you find difficult to bring to God? Do you find yourself doubting that he's able to change your situation? Begin to pray about one such need, despite your doubts.*

Come and see what God has done, how awesome his works in man's behalf!
He turned the sea into dry land, they passed through the waters on foot—come,
let us rejoice in him. He rules forever by his power.

PSALM 66:5-7

I used to make excuses for my faint-hearted prayer life. But God convinced me that I was not being honest with myself. The real reason my prayers were weak was that my faith was weak. In my heart, I did not believe that God could do anything about the messes all around me.

I decided I didn't want to stay where I was, essentially disbelieving God's omnipotence. So I launched an assault on my own lack of conviction. I located almost every biblical passage that emphasized God's ability to accomplish anything he desires.

The verses I read affirmed what I already knew: God is capable of handling any problem we could bring him. Creating planets isn't much of a problem for him. Neither is raising the dead. Nothing is too difficult for God to handle— but he's waiting for us to recognize his power and ask for his help.

JOURNAL: *Write a letter to God, admitting the places where your faith is weak. Notice what it does to your relationship with God and your desire to replace those doubts with truth.*

God's Power over Circumstances

Suddenly an angel of the Lord appeared. . . . "Quick, get up!" he said,
and the chains fell off Peter's wrists. . . . They passed [the guards] and came to the iron gate
leading to the city. It opened for them by itself, and they went through it.

ACTS 12:7, 10

Imagine Peter after he's been sprung from jail by an angel. Baffled, he looked around him. Was this real? Was he free? Had an angel really opened those prison doors? When the truth dawned on him, he made a beeline for the gathered believers.

A servant girl answered his knock. Hearing his voice, she ran back to tell the praying saints that their prayers were answered.

"You're out of your mind," they told her. When she kept insisting that it was so, they said, "It must be his angel."

But Peter kept on knocking, and when they opened the door and saw him, they were astonished (vv. 15-16).

The first Christians were no more inclined than contemporary Christians to think that God would miraculously rearrange circumstances in answer to prayer, but they prayed anyway. And God rewarded their somewhat incomplete faith—not by sending them comforting visions but by altering history.

APPLY: *What circumstances are you facing right now that need not just "comforting visions" but God's power to help? Where in your life do you need to trust and "keep knocking"?*

Our Immutable God

I the LORD do not change.

MALACHI 3:6

Jesus Christ is the same yesterday and today and forever.

HEBREWS 13:8

God's immutability is firmly established by biblical passages like these. God has not changed. He is not growing old, and his power is not waning.

As I sought to strengthen my prayer life, I studied passages like these. I didn't want simply to agree with the doctrine of God's omnipotence (I already did that); I wanted to own it, which is a different matter all together. I wanted to be able to say, "I don't care what other people think. I don't care about scholars' opinions. I believe that God has shown his omnipotence in history."

But it's one thing to own the doctrine of God's omnipotence in history; it's quite another to own the doctrine of his omnipotence today, in my hometown, over my problems and concerns. To believe this, I must believe that God does not change, that he is immutable.

JOURNAL: *List some attributes of God that you've seen in your own life: perhaps his faithfulness, his strength, his goodness. Reflect on the fact that these attributes will not change, even if your circumstances do. Write God a letter of thankfulness for his immutability.*

Power to Change Us

"Simon, Simon," [Jesus said to Peter, the very night of the arrest and denial,]
"Satan has asked to sift you as wheat.
But I have prayed for you, Simon, that your faith may not fail.
And when you have turned back, strengthen your brothers."

LUKE 22:31-32

When Jesus was captured in the middle of the night and dragged before religious and civil authorities, most of the disciples ran away in terror. Peter, to his credit, followed his Master right into the high priest's courtyard. But there he lost heart. "They're going to kill him," he thought, "and then they'll start looking for his friends." And so Peter, fearing for his life even though no one had threatened it, unsuccessfully tried to persuade a group of servants that he had no connections with Jesus.

Jesus knew Peter would deny him, and he also knew that Peter the coward, through God's mighty power, would become Peter the rock, the first major leader of the Christian church (Matthew 16:18-19). After the crucifixion, Peter was a broken man. He couldn't put the pieces back together by himself. Only God's power could change him. And it did.

PRAY: *In which areas of your life are you tempted to give in to fear or lose heart? Ask God to release his power, change your heart and give you the courage to face whatever you are facing.*

M O N D A Y *Love Is Tender and Tough*

> *Be kind to one another, tenderhearted, forgiving one another,*
> *as God in Christ has forgiven you.*

EPHESIANS 4:32 NRSV

For many of us, this is not an easy command to follow. Tenderness seems to be a reflex reaction to some people, but for others it is alien and difficult. You see this in public places like airports and shopping centers. An elderly woman is struggling with luggage or packages, and a steady stream of able-bodied people pass her by. Some even scowl and say, "Get a move on, Grandma." And then a tenderhearted person comes along and takes time to help her.

There are many reasons why some people are tender while others are tough. Part of it can be explained as God's workmanship. He makes us all different. Part of it is due to family heritage, the individual's temperament and the kind of experiences he or she has had. Both tenderness and toughness are important character qualities; both are necessary sides of love.

JOURNAL: *Write about a tenderhearted action that you took. Was it yesterday, or last year? Write about what circumstances have made you either tender or tough.*

Tough and Tender Hearts

As water reflects a face, so a man's heart reflects the man.

PROVERBS 27:19

A huge plant in our living room got a disease, and my wife, worried that it would infect other plants in our house, decided to dispose of it. One morning while the children were at school, she hacked all the branches off and loaded them in garbage bags. She left the big pot with the plant's stump in the living room so that, when I got home, I could carry it out to the garage.

In the afternoon our kids went into the living room and saw the pot. Our son, who was then six, burst into tears. "Why did you do such an awful thing?" he asked Lynne. "Did you have to kill the plant? Did it hurt when the plant died?"

Meanwhile our daughter, age nine, said disgustedly, "Todd, it was only a sick old house plant. Don't worry about it. I'm glad Mom chopped it down and put it out of its misery."

Two children born of the same parents, raised in the same family with the same levels of love—but one was being a lot more tender than the other. God gives us different personalities, each with unique strengths and weaknesses.

APPLY: *Does your heart tend to be more tough, or tender? What do you see as the strengths and weaknesses of either type of personality?*

A Heart of Stone?

I will give you a new heart and put a new spirit in you;
I will remove from you your heart of stone and give you a heart of flesh.

EZEKIEL 36:26

If we harder-hearted Christians are honest and courageous, we have to admit that our tough approach can do damage. We kid people that we shouldn't kid, and when they get hurt we say, "Can't you take a joke?" We don't listen to other people very well. Usually while they are talking to us we are either making unrelated plans or mentally responding to what they are saying. We wonder why many people are so weak and timid. We use people and dispose of them unceremoniously when they have served our purposes. Although we may not realize it, others tell us we act superior. We love to be right, to compete and especially to win.

But in our moments of quiet reflection—which usually come only when we've been brought low by a financial setback, an accident, an illness, a divorce or some other crisis—we don't like what we see in our souls. But thankfully, we serve a God who is able to change us and soften our hearts.

PRAY: *Reflect on the condition of your heart. If you tend to be hardhearted, courageously pray that God will fulfill his promise in Ezekiel to give you a new heart.*

I will give them a heart to know me, that I am the LORD.
They will be my people, and I will be their God,
for they will return to me with all their heart.

JEREMIAH 24:7

If we are in a saving relationship with Jesus Christ, God is already at work on our hearts. For the tough ones among us, he's got his work cut out for him. During my own rare times of introspection, I have asked myself, "How can my heart be so hard? I've experienced the personal love of Jesus Christ firsthand. His love has marked my soul and changed me. I know the Holy Spirit resides in my life and is working me over from the inside out, trying to make me a more loving man. I know that God has graciously put me in charge of a community of brothers and sisters who are growing in their attempt to become more loving people. But I'm still too callous and cold. What more is required for me to become tenderhearted? What practical steps can I take to relate to people in a more tender fashion?" Believe it or not, sometimes it takes more courage to be tender than tough.

APPLY: *What steps can you take to relate to others in a tender way? What fears or habits keep you from showing tenderness?*

FRIDAY

And now these three remain: faith, hope and love.
But the greatest of these is love.

1 CORINTHIANS 13:13

The greatest legacy we humans can leave is the legacy of love. Whether we're speaking of our place within society at large or in the context of our primary relationships, the most valuable gifts we can offer are those thoughts and actions that flow from a loving heart.

It is within the context of family that loving actions are most appreciated and necessary—and most difficult to maintain. We all have good intentions, but in the rough-and-tumble events of life we tend to bump and bruise each other. Even little wounds to our egos or our souls hurt, and often our natural reaction is to withdraw.

As emotional distance increases, so does resentment. We know we should put an end to the discord. We should talk to the other person and try to resolve the problem. But we know how much time and energy it will take and how frustrating it may be.

Don't get lazy and give up. Make the phone call. Write the letter. Take initiative in pursuing reconciliation or a deeper relationship. Don't take the destructive path of the sluggard. Instead, leave a legacy of love.

PRAY: *Ask God to show you where you have bumped and bruised those you love. Ask for his help to pursue reconciliation.*

SATURDAY/SUNDAY

Jesus' Love Has Power

When they came to the place called the Skull, there they crucified him,
along with the criminals—one on his right, the other on his left.
Jesus said, "Father, forgive them, for they do not know what they are doing."

LUKE 23:33-34

Jesus showed radical love all his life. At the end he took slaps without saying anything. He absorbed beatings without cursing anyone. When nails were pounded into his hands and feet, he did not turn to the people doing the pounding and say, "You're going to rot in hell for this!" No, he said, "Father, these men matter to you. Don't charge this crime to their account. Forgive them. They don't know what they're doing."

As Jesus died, a Clint Eastwood kind of man, a hardened Roman officer, broke down and cried, "Surely this was the Son of God!" I doubt if the soldier had ever heard any theology, but he was broken by the power of Jesus' radical, nonretaliatory, second-mile love. If we want to build a courageous faith, we need to ask God to help us love in that same radical way.

JOURNAL: *Write about a time when you were broken by the power of Jesus' radical, tender love for you. Write about some ways you might be able to show that love to others.*

MONDAY

Tough Love

> *Woe to you, teachers of the law and Pharisees, you hypocrites! . . .*
> *You are like whitewashed tombs, which look beautiful on the outside but on the*
> *inside are full of dead men's bones and everything unclean. . . .*
> *You snakes! You brood of vipers! How will you escape being condemned to hell?*

MATTHEW 23:13, 27, 33

You probably recognize these words of Jesus, the gentle Shepherd, the tenderhearted, meek and lowly Savior. How could he talk so tough to people he claimed to love? Why did he say these hard words?

Jesus said these things because they were true. His words were upsetting, difficult to receive, tough to swallow—but true. Quite often the truth must simply be told straight out, with no room for confusion or misinterpretation, to avoid the greater damage of living by lies. Jesus had an overwhelming concern for the people he was addressing. He loved them, and he wanted them to come to grips with the truth before they shipwrecked their lives and jeopardized eternity. Jesus was demonstrating tough love—a kind of love that is usually painful but very potent. In certain situations, we're called to follow his example. Careful use of tough love not only challenges others, but grows us up as well.

JOURNAL: *Write about a time you were confronted by someone who cared for you. What did it feel like to be the recipient of tough love?*

T U E S D A Y

Pleasing People, or God?

Am I now trying to win the approval of men, or of God? . . .
If I were still trying to please men, I would not be a servant of Christ.

GALATIANS 1:10

To tenderhearted people, tough love sounds frightening and maybe even unchristian. It comes easier to those of us who are by nature tougher hearted. When we see a problem in the life of someone we love, we do not hesitate to say, "What we need here is surgery. Let's hack through his surface-level excuses with a scalpel and get right to the heart of the matter. If it causes a little bleeding, that's okay as long as the problem gets fixed. If he survives the surgery, he'll thank us later."

Hearing this, tenderhearted people panic and say to themselves, "Surgery? Scalpel? Blood? I never want to see that happen to anyone, let alone do it myself. All I want is peace and harmony. Maybe with enough hugs, the problems will solve themselves." To you tenderhearted people, God would say, "I understand your tender spirit—I made you that way. But if you're going to learn how to really love, you're going to have to sometimes get tough." Sometimes courageous faith means giving up people pleasing.

APPLY: *Do you worry more about pleasing people or pleasing God? What would it take for you to love in a strong or tough way?*

Living in the Light

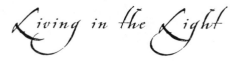

For you were once darkness, but now you are light in the Lord.
Live as children of light (for the fruit of the light consists in all goodness,
righteousness and truth) and find out what pleases the Lord.
Have nothing to do with the fruitless deeds of darkness, but rather expose them.

EPHESIANS 5:8-11

One of my colleagues is a true-blue charter member of the tender hearts club. He says he knew nothing about tough love until recent years when some of his Christian brothers demonstrated tough love to him in a lot of ticklish areas in his life. Once, when he heard I was preparing a sermon on tough love, he wrote me this note: "Tell those tenderhearted people that if my brothers hadn't demonstrated tough love to me, I wouldn't have a growing relationship with my wife, an effective ministry, a disciplined walk with Christ, a righteous hatred of sin, respect for the people I lead, my debts paid and money in the bank. But because of tough love, I have all those things. Everybody needs tough-love lessons." Those tough-love lessons help us live as children of light.

PRAY: *Recall times that someone has demonstrated tough love in your life. Thank God for the benefits this has brought to your life. Pray that God will help you live in his light.*

Growing Up

Then we will no longer be infants . . .
blown here and there by every wind of teaching and by the
cunning and craftiness of men in their deceitful scheming.
Instead, speaking the truth in love, we will in all things grow up into
him who is the Head, that is, Christ.

EPHESIANS 4:14-15

Everywhere I look I see people who need to experience tough love. I see married couples on the edge of serious trouble, young people pushing their luck to the limits, all kinds of people wandering aimlessly in the wastelands of destructive pleasure seeking.

But somebody has to have the courage to tell these people they're on a merry-go-round going nowhere. Somebody has to shake them and say, "God has a better way for you. Look to him for direction." Somebody has to say, "I love you too much to watch you shipwreck your life, your marriage, your family, your job, your soul. So sit down and listen to me, because I'm going to say some hard things to you. I don't like doing this, but I must because I love you too much to stay silent when I see you hurting yourself." Speaking truth often helps people to grow up.

A P P L Y : *In what area(s) of your life are you on a merry-go-round? Have you been willing to listen to someone who's confronted you and wanted to help you grow?*

Peace at Any Price?

They dress the wound of my people as though it were not serious.
"Peace, peace," they say, when there is no peace.

JEREMIAH 8:11

Tenderhearted people will go to unbelievable lengths to avoid any kind of turmoil in a relationship. If there's a little tension in the marriage and one partner asks the other, "What's wrong?" the tender one will answer, "Nothing." What he or she is really saying is this: "Something's wrong, but I don't want to make a scene." In choosing peacekeeping over truth telling, these people think they are being noble, but in reality they are making a bad choice. Whatever caused the tension will come back. The peace will get harder and harder to keep. A spirit of disappointment will start to flow through the peacekeeper's veins, leading first to anger, then to bitterness and finally to hatred. Relationships can die while everything looks peaceful on the surface!

Peace at any price is a form of deception. When you know you need to tell the truth, the evil one whispers in your ear, "Don't do it. He won't listen. She won't take it. It will only make things worse." If you believe those lies, you will probably kill your relationship sooner or later. Tell the truth!

PRAY: *Are you ignoring serious wounds in a relationship that need to be tended? Pray for the courage to speak the truth, even if it's uncomfortable.*

Speak Truth

Therefore, putting away falsehood, let every one speak the truth with his neighbor,
for we are members one of another.

EPHESIANS 4:25 RSV

This command, which the Lord gave through Paul as he wrote to the young church at Ephesus, makes tenderhearted people tremble to their bones. He tells us that first, we are to stop lying to each other. Second, we are to speak the truth—"in love," Paul says in verse 15. This verse reminds us of a truth about deep relationships: the well-being of the other person is more important than the current comfort level in the relationship.

Someone's well-being and their comfort are not the same things. It takes courage to speak the truth when we know that doing so will make waves and rock canoes. But any approach other than truth telling, over time, will undermine the integrity of our relationships. A relationship built on peacekeeping won't last. Tough love chooses truth telling over peacekeeping and trusts God for the outcome. Truth telling builds relationships that will endure.

APPLY: *Are you currently in a relationship that's built on peacekeeping, but ignoring the truth? Are you trying to keep someone comfortable, but feeling a lot of discomfort about it? Take a step toward truth telling.*

M O N D A Y
Risk Discomfort

> *I am astonished that you are so quickly deserting the one who called you*
> *by the grace of Christ and are turning to a different gospel—*
> *which is really no gospel at all. Evidently some people are throwing you into confusion*
> *and are trying to pervert the gospel of Christ.*

GALATIANS 1:6-7

One of the best definitions of tough love I know is *action for the well-being of the beloved.* We need to love others with such devotion that we will risk our comfort level in order to protect the other person's well-being.

I once told a friend, "I'm not trying to run your life, but I'm concerned about the direction it's taking." He was so angry that he came close to leaping over the table to punch my lights out. So, man of valor that I am, I said, "Sorry, I'll never mention this again." I didn't, either, and he shipwrecked his life. I still see this friend occasionally, and many times I've said to him, "I failed you. I should have said, 'Leap over that table and deck me, if it will make you feel any better, but I'm going to tell you again that I'm concerned about your future.'" Maybe God would have used me if I had been a little more tenacious.

JOURNAL: *Write about a time when you should have told the truth to someone but didn't. In retrospect, what would you do differently?*

Don't Avoid

If your brother sins against you, go and show him his fault, just between the two of you.
If he listens to you, you have won your brother over.

MATTHEW 18:15

Most of us prefer to avoid confrontation. We have a strong aversion to the very vehicle God has appointed to restore true peace between people!

Whenever you take action on behalf of another person's well-being, you are taking a big risk. The comfort level between you may drop precipitously. Over time, however, the outcome of speaking the truth in love—especially when the relationship is basically mature and healthy—is usually positive. The obstacle in your relationship turns into a building block, and the two of you reach new understandings, make new commitments and establish deeper trust. But we all know that it is much easier to write and read about tough love than actually to sit down and have a heart-to-heart talk with someone. Confronting people can be frightening, but God promises to be with us and help us as we do it.

APPLY: *Are you the type who avoids confrontation and internalizes frustration? Pay attention to the way you relate to people, and see if you can use healthy confrontation, when appropriate, to build stronger relationships.*

The Banana Room

Settle matters quickly with your adversary who is taking you to court.
Do it while you are still with him on the way.

MATTHEW 5:25

Even when I was a little boy I noticed that, whenever a problem had to be worked out between two employees at my dad's produce company, they would go into "the banana room." Sometimes my dad or one of the other owners would say to someone, "I need to see you in the banana room." Sometimes a foreman would grab a dockworker and they would disappear in there.

The banana room was a temperature-controlled room containing up to eight hundred cases of bananas. It was completely enclosed and had a four-inch steel door, so no one outside could hear what was going on inside. Maybe that is why, when a summons to the banana room came, everybody quaked. "Oh no—not the banana room!" No one ever died in the banana room, and a lot of times after a discussion in there, people would come out smiling, with their arms around each other. Still, people feared that room. Resolving relational conflicts takes face-to-face, heart-to-heart discussions. That can be terrifying, but it's often how God builds our character.

PRAY: *How do you feel about face-to-face, heart-to-heart discussions? Do you fear initiating them, or being on the receiving end? Pray for the courage to go into such discussions with an open heart and mind.*

Preparation Helps

> *Love must be sincere. Hate what is evil; cling to what is good.*
> *Be devoted to one another in brotherly love.*
> *Honor one another above yourselves.*

ROMANS 12:9-10

When you prepare properly for a confrontation, you have won half the battle. You win the other half when you conduct the heart-to-heart talk sensitively. It's important that you present your concerns clearly. While these steps won't guarantee heartfelt thanks and warm fuzzies all around, they will give you the best possible chance of being listened to and respected.

First, begin with a sincere statement of commitment to the relationship. If you're talking to your spouse, tell him or her that your marriage is the most important relationship in the world to you and that you want it to get even better. If you're talking to a friend, tell him or her how much you appreciate the friendship. If you're in a work situation, tell your supervisor that you enjoy working for her, or your employee that you're glad he's on your team. In all cases, let the person you're talking to know that you're not issuing ultimatums—you're just trying to work on a problem. And ultimately, you're trying to improve a relationship.

APPLY: *How do you prepare for confrontation? What happens to a conversation when you start with a statement of sincere commitment?*

Ministry of Reconciliation

> *All this is from God, who reconciled us to himself through Christ*
> *and gave us the ministry of reconciliation:*
> *that God was reconciling the world to himself in Christ,*
> *not counting men's sins against them.*
> *And he has committed to us the message of reconciliation.*

2 CORINTHIANS 5:18-19

When you are confronting someone, make a careful, nonaccusatory explanation of the issue as you see it. Avoid saying "you always" or "you never." State the problem as carefully as you know how, using "I feel" statements whenever possible.

Also, invite dialogue. After you have spilled your heart on the matter, ask, "Am I out to lunch on this? Do I have my facts straight? Am I missing something? Am I overly sensitive?" As a pastor, I am frequently challenged and confronted. When I sense in the challenger an open invitation to discuss the point, usually something can be worked out. But if someone finishes off an accusation by saying, in effect, "So there—I will allow you one phone call before I sentence you to an untimely death," I feel defensive. Be fair, invite dialogue, and watch God transform conflicts into opportunities for growth and reconciliation.

JOURNAL: *Write about this: what does it mean to have a ministry of reconciliation? How might a person committed to reconciliation go about confronting someone?*

Confronting Is a Process

A man has his father's wife. And you are proud! Shouldn't you rather have been filled with grief and have put out of your fellowship the man who did this?

1 CORINTHIANS 5:1-2

When Paul confronted the church at Corinth about some flagrant immorality, do you think the recipients of his admonishment said, "Thank you very much for bringing this to our attention"? Likewise, when you confront, you might get a slammed door, a pink slip or an earful of angry words. But if your relationship is built on deception, you are in big trouble already. So take the risk, make some waves and see what God does.

Most probably, the person will eventually take your words seriously, and your relationship will once again stand on firm ground. It is hard to resist someone who is humble and vulnerable. This may not happen immediately, however. Sometimes it takes several confrontations before the process is complete, and sometimes a relationship gets worse before it gets better. Some people excuse continuing hostilities by saying, "Well, I tried to patch it up once, and the other person wouldn't listen." But it is unrealistic to expect one hour to undo the work of six months, or ten years. Trust that God's timing is perfect, and his work continues even if you can't see it.

APPLY: *Have you tried to reconcile a relationship and it hasn't worked? What's keeping you from trying again?*

MONDAY *Mediation Can Help*

If your brother sins against you, go and show him his fault,
just between the two of you. . . . But if he will not listen, take one or two others along. . . .
If he refuses to listen to them, tell it to the church; and if he refuses to listen even to the church,
treat him as you would a pagan or a tax collector.

MATTHEW 18:15-17

Unfortunately, despite your best efforts, sometimes the person refuses to listen. In that case, bring in someone you both trust and respect, and let this person help you communicate. Your church may be able to help you find a mediator—the pastor, a small-group leader, an elder. Or you may wish to discuss your problems with a professional counselor, especially when alcohol or drug abuse is involved. Mediation may bring good results you cannot obtain on your own.

But we might as well face the facts—in some cases, tough love brings on permanent division. For whatever reasons, sometimes the two of you will separate and go your own ways. When relationships are terminated, it breaks God's heart. But sometimes that is life in this sinful world; when it happens, we confess our sins, pick ourselves up and, by God's grace, we go on.

PRAY: *If you are trying to confront someone who refuses to listen, pray about finding someone who can act as a mediator.*

Don't Give Up

If someone is caught in a sin, you who are spiritual should restore him gently.
But watch yourself, or you also may be tempted.
Carry each other's burdens, and in this way you will fulfill the law of Christ.

GALATIANS 6:1-2

Too many of us give up without a fight when a relationship begins to disintegrate. We scrap and claw and even go to court to protect our property, but all we do is cry a little when relationships die. This is backward thinking. Relationships are worth fighting for. Love needs to be tough enough to hang on. Jesus' love for us is the tenderest love we will ever know. He died to heal our sins and to give us eternal life with him. He guides us, protects us, comforts us and nourishes us with his Word. But Jesus' love is also the toughest love we will ever face. He knows our hearts and does not hesitate to tell us when he finds sin there. He loves us too much to allow us to continue unchecked down a path of self-destruction.

Real love is always both tender and tough. May God give us the sensitivity to know when to show each kind of love and the courage to do whatever love demands.

APPLY: *What steps could you take to fight for the survival of a disintegrating relationship? Resolve to do what it takes to follow Christ in your relationships.*

Be Prepared

> *Be prepared in season and out of season;*
> *correct, rebuke and encourage—with great patience and careful instruction.*
> *For the time will come when men will not put up with sound doctrine. . . .*
> *They will turn their ears away from the truth and turn aside to myths.*
> *But you, keep your head in all situations.*

2 TIMOTHY 4:2-5

When a given situation demands that a word of truth be spoken, we are commanded to speak it without hesitating, without holding back and without considering the cost to ourselves, even if it costs us dearly.

For me, this is the growing edge of my abilities in truth telling. By God's grace, at this point in my life I have little temptation to fabricate wild webs of deception or to create sinister shadings of truth; as I consciously monitor my words for honesty, I sense God's affirmation of my growth in this area. But when it comes to saying the hard truths that certain people desperately need to hear, I too often find myself hesitating. By speaking up, I give God an opportunity to build my faith and strengthen my character.

A P P L Y : *Is there someone who needs you to correct, rebuke or encourage them? Is there someone in your life who has turned away from truth and needs you to guide them back?*

Don't Hold Back Truth

Brothers, if someone is caught in a sin, you who are spiritual should restore him gently.
But watch yourself, or you also may be tempted.

GALATIANS 6:1

I have a friend who is slowly destroying his oldest child. The father is a high-control person who is determined to turn his sixteen-year-old son into a star athlete. But the kid isn't interested in athletics; anyone (except his father, apparently) can see his passion and talent for writing and performing music. Predictably, their relationship is deteriorating. The dad keeps adding athletic pressure; the son keeps pulling away.

Why do I stay silent? Why haven't I told the truth to that dad? Why haven't I carefully described what I discern about his son and about the destructive patterns of control I see in the family? I've proven my love and respect for my friend in many ways during the years of our friendship; he knows I have his best interests at heart. Yet I am afraid to speak the truth. I pray for courage to obey God's command to restore others by telling the truth.

P R A Y : *If there is a situation where you are afraid to speak truth, talk to God about it. Ask him for the courage to speak up, and the wisdom to say words that will be appropriate.*

FRIDAY

Trading Truth for Tranquility

> *Do not let kindness and truth leave you; bind them around your neck,*
> *write them on the tablet of your heart.*

PROVERBS 3:3 NASB

Most of us shrink back from telling the truth because it might cost us something. It might create discomfort in the relationship. We might be misunderstood or rejected.

Too often I choose peacekeeping over truth telling. I silence words of truth because they might create ripples on the pond of my life, and I, like many people, am a tranquility junkie. I want smooth waters, not rough seas. That's the truth about me, and I hate it.

We must doggedly cling to the truth no matter what, and not only cling to it but also reveal it to others who need to know it. Do you find it hard to do this? Then write the truth on the tablet of your heart so you can't miss it, and hang a necklace of truth around your neck so no one else can miss it either. Cling to the truth and reveal the truth—in your marriage and family, in your friendships, in your school or marketplace relationships, and in the church. It may cost us something, but it will be worth it.

JOURNAL: *Write some things you would say to those you love if you were able to be honest with them. Pick one thing you've written and resolve to share it.*

Listen to Earnest Counsel

Perfume and incense bring joy to the heart,
and the pleasantness of one's friend springs from his earnest counsel.

PROVERBS 27:9

A close friend of mine once said to me, "I think it's time for you to get some Christian counseling. I know you pray a lot. I know you read the Bible and apply it to your life. But it seems to me that there is a brokenness inside of you that you probably won't be able to fix without the help of a wise, caring, Christian counselor."

I did not like hearing those words. "Hey, buddy," I wanted to scream in his face, "don't you go telling me I need a counselor." Of course, my response was a huge indicator of my need for internal work, but I didn't see that at the time. What I saw was that I was a picture of health in every way, and he had no business implying otherwise.

Years after the fact, I am so thankful that this man was willing to pay the price for telling me the truth. I desperately needed to hear it. Cling to the truth and reveal the truth. You have no idea how God might choose to use your words to transform a human life.

PRAY: *Whom do you need to give earnest counsel to? Ask God to give you an opportunity to speak the truth in love to that person.*

MONDAY *Opportunity for Growth*

> *Let us not give up meeting together, as some are in the habit of doing,*
> *but let us encourage one another.*

HEBREWS 10:25

Coming together, whether for formal church services or more informal small-group gatherings, is not about following some legalistic rule; it is about taking advantage of a significant means of spiritual growth. You and I never know when God is going to show up at a particular gathering of Christians in such a powerful and personal way that it touches our hearts and transforms us on the inside. If we take a casual approach to gathering together, we are setting ourselves up to miss out on the potential work of God in our lives.

During my lifetime, I have sat through many church services and small-group meetings during which it seemed as though nothing special was happening inside of me. But I have also sat through similar services and meetings during which my heart was turned inside out and my life was turned around. There was no way to know ahead of time when God would choose to use the gathering of Christians to touch me in a unique and powerful way.

PRAY: *Have you been consistent in gathering with other believers? Confess to God, if appropriate, and ask for his help in obeying this command.*

Finding Friendships

> *Bear with each other and forgive whatever grievances you may have against one another.*
> *Forgive as the Lord forgave you. And over all these virtues put on love,*
> *which binds them all together in perfect unity.*

COLOSSIANS 3:13-14

How can we build meaningful friendships? I often hear people complain that they don't have any close friends, but that is usually because they have failed to take disciplined action to establish such relationships. They don't have the courage to follow what Colossians 3 says and be gracious and forgiving. A disciplined person would say, "I am going to make a major decision to get involved in a small group of fellow Christians where other people will be looking for friends too, and I am going to follow through on that decision. Then, every time the group meets, I am going to show up and open up and build some friendships." In a year or eighteen months, that man or woman probably will be able to look around a dining room table and see four or five people who have become like brothers and sisters—thanks to an advance decision. Doing the hard work of relationship building results in deep joy and life-giving companionship.

APPLY: *What does it mean to forgive as the Lord forgave you? How would such a practice relate to the discipline of building meaningful friendships?*

Choosing Wise Friends

*Let us consider how we may spur one another on toward love and good deeds.
Let us not give up meeting together, as some are in the habit of doing,
but let us encourage one another.*

HEBREWS 10:24-25

If we are committed to following God's path, if we want to hold on to our hope in Christ, if we want to grow in wisdom, initiative, goodness, discipline, truth and so on, then we should intentionally surround ourselves with people who exhibit those qualities.

Choosing the right friends is like putting together our own personal development team; it will greatly enhance our efforts in moving forward on the right path. If we want to develop sober judgment, we should choose friends renowned for making wise decisions. If we want to strengthen our convictions, we should pick people with reputations for standing up for what they believe. If we wish we were kinder, we should spend more time with those who treat others with gentleness and grace. If we want to walk more closely with God, we should put ourselves under the influence of people who make spiritual disciplines a priority. As our friendships with those people grow, so will our character and our pursuit of godliness.

PRAY: *Ask God for wisdom in choosing friends who can aid your personal development and "spur you on toward love and good deeds"—and for whom you can do the same.*

Choosing Companions Wisely

He who walks with the wise grows wise, but a companion of fools suffers harm.

PROVERBS 13:20

While Proverbs exhorts us to walk through life with godly companions, it also offers some words of warning about walking through life with friends. Yes, we all ought to walk closely with a few friends. But we need to be very careful, says the writer of this proverb, about whom we choose as friends. Wise friends will make us wise; foolish friends will bring us harm.

According to this proverb, close friends are more deeply connected than we might think. Though we may view ourselves as independent individuals, we are joined to our close friends by something akin to permeable membranes, those ultrathin walls through which tiny particles can pass back and forth. What passes between close friends are values, convictions, morals, habits and goals. They pass back and forth whether we realize it or not, so despite our illusions of individuality, we end up being deeply affected by either the wisdom or the foolishness of our friends. That's why we need to choose our friends wisely.

JOURNAL: *Write about a time when a foolish friend brought you harm. What did you learn from that experience? What steps can you take to choose your friends wisely?*

FRIDAY

Avoiding Foolish Friends

*Have nothing to do with the fruitless deeds of darkness, but rather expose them. . . .
Therefore do not be foolish, but understand what the Lord's will is.*

EPHESIANS 5:11, 17

Just as wise friends can help us, foolish friends can ruin us. Their folly can seep into our lives and taint our desires and goals. Their faulty moral compasses can steer us off course. Their distortions of truth can undermine our understanding of God and his ways. If we let ourselves be corrupted, we'll pay; as Proverbs says, we'll "suffer harm." I know this is true; I've heard a thousand variations on this theme. It is uncanny how often people whose lives aren't working well can trace their downfall back to the choice they made to forge a friendship with a foolish person. What kind of people are your closest friends?

JOURNAL: *Write down the names of your closest friends. Then write about their character: Are they wise or foolish? Do they walk closely with God or are they "ignorant of God"? Write honestly about how they influence you.*

No Exception to the Rule

Do not be misled: "Bad company corrupts good character."
Come back to your senses as you ought, and stop sinning;
for there are some who are ignorant of God—I say this to your shame.

1 CORINTHIANS 15:33-34

As I listen to people who tell me how their growth was hindered by the bad influence of their friends, I try to convince myself that I am different from them, an exception to the rule. I try to tell myself that I have walked with God long enough and have become stable enough and can hear the whisper of the Holy Spirit clearly enough that I could spend any amount of time with any kind of person and remain unaffected. I would like to think that. But when Paul wrote to the Corinthians, "Do not be misled," he was also writing to me. If I think I am an exception to this rule, I have been misled and deceived. I, like anyone else, will become like the people I choose to be close to. That's why I don't make that choice lightly.

APPLY: *Take time for some honest self-assessment. Are your closest friends people you would like to emulate? Do you think that your friends won't have an influence on you? Are you misled?*

M O N D A Y *Recognizing Red Flags*

There are six things the LORD hates, seven that are detestable to him:
haughty eyes, a lying tongue, hands that shed innocent blood,
a heart that devises wicked schemes, feet that are quick to rush into evil,
a false witness who pours out lies and a man who stirs up dissension among brothers.

PROVERBS 6:16-19

Whenever we see any of these characteristics in a person, we ought to have red flags going up everywhere. This is not the kind of person we should count among our intimate circle of friends. Again, this does not mean we should deem such a person insignificant to us or to God; it does mean, however, that we should never give him or her a position of influence in our lives.

Of course, men or women who exhibit the traits described in this passage still matter to God. We should use every opportunity we have to touch their lives in a positive way; we should be kind to them, serve them, love them and patiently point them toward the love of God and the gospel of grace, forgiveness and reconciliation. But they are not the people we should invite to walk closely with us through life.

P R A Y : *Ask God to help you develop discernment so that you can recognize the red flags warning you to steer clear of potentially destructive relationships.*

Avoid Evildoers

> *Do not envy wicked men, do not desire their company;*
> *for their hearts plot violence, and their lips talk about making trouble.*

PROVERBS 24:1-2

I met with a Christian leader who had devoted his life to trying to shut down the producers and distributors of pornography. After hearing about his work, I asked him what kind of person would build a career in pornography, particularly child pornography.

He said, "You'd be amazed at what people can justify. In the pornography industry, film directors call what's going on in the beds 'acting.' The government turns the other way and calls it 'art.' Producers and distributors call it 'free enterprise.' Video stores call it 'entertainment.' The consumers who buy this junk call it 'a good night of fun.' But while all of this evil rationalization is going on, thousands of children's minds and bodies are being abused and destroyed."

You may avoid pornographers as friends. But what about the man who develops a business plan that borders on illegality? Or what about the woman who includes personal expenses on her expense account at work? Do you want people like that on your personal development team? Seek out honorable friends.

PRAY: *Do you have friends whose ethics you question? Ask God to help you set boundaries so those friends don't influence your decisions, and to help you develop friendships with people who model ethical behavior.*

A Haughty Spirit

Pride goes before destruction, a haughty spirit before a fall.

PROVERBS 16:18

What does it mean to be "haughty"? This refers to someone with an attitude of superiority, someone who says, even if only with his or her eyes, "I have value; you are worthless. I am a winner; you are a loser. I am a professional; you are a blue-collar worker. I am educated; you are a dropout. I am beautiful; you are plain. I am married; you are single. I am conservative; you are liberal. I am a career woman; you are a stay-at-home mom. I am spiritually mature; you are not." (Many of these pairs could be reversed; haughty eyes can look both ways.)

Such arrogance is frequently denounced in Scripture, and one who exhibits it receives a dire prediction for the future. Do you want companions headed for destruction? Walking partners destined to fall? Then steer clear of people with haughty eyes. Do not let their view of life color your view, and do not let their future become yours. Haughtiness, it seems, can be contagious.

JOURNAL: *Write about a time you encountered someone with a haughty spirit. How did you feel? Why might a haughty spirit be especially contagious?*

Don't Treat Truth Lightly

*If [sinners] say, "Come along with us; . . . we will get all sorts of valuable things
and fill our houses with plunder," . . . do not go along with them.*

PROVERBS 1 : 1 1 - 1 5

If we walk with people who treat the truth lightly, we run the risk of becoming that way ourselves. A small-group leader in our youth ministry recently told me of a family ripped apart by the lies of a teenage son.

When he was fifteen, this young man became involved with a group of students who told "little lies" to their parents—cover-ups about where they were going and what they were doing. At first he felt uncomfortable, but eventually he began to see this practice as a harmless shading of reality that normal kids always do.

Once truth became negotiable in his mind, he eventually broke trust with everyone—parents, girlfriend, teachers. Not only did his blanket of lies hide a lifestyle of drug abuse and petty theft that landed him in deep legal difficulties, but also it forced him into the long and agonizing process of rebuilding relational trust.

If you walk with people who don't tell the truth, you may be headed for heartache. Choose friends wisely.

A P P L Y : *Have you ever gone down a path of destruction, led by people you thought were friends? What can you learn from those mistakes?*

Strife Spreading

A perverse man spreads strife.
PROVERBS 16:28 NASB

Blessed are the peacemakers, for they will be called sons of God.
MATTHEW 5:9

Have you ever tried to have a relationship with someone who has a habit of nursing grudges, demands huge apologies or has a chronically unforgiving spirit? Avoid such people.

Why is spreading strife perverse? Because any person who has been miraculously reconciled to God through the work of Jesus Christ has received the Holy Spirit, and in receiving the Holy Spirit, that person has also received the spirit of reconciliation. Anytime a problem arises in a relationship, the Spirit of God starts whispering to that person, "Let's not blow this up. Let's resolve this quickly." Anyone who claims to be a follower of Christ but enjoys spreading strife has chosen not to listen to the voice of reconciliation that speaks within, and has deliberately turned away from what is right.

Such a person delights in dwelling on disputes and alienating friends and can have no lasting place among people who want to walk together through life. Which would you rather have on your team? One who spreads strife among friends or one who is a peacemaker? One whom the Bible calls perverse or one whom Jesus calls blessed? It's ours to choose.

APPLY: *Whose influence are you subjecting your life to? What changes should you think about making?*

Relational Integrity

As iron sharpens iron, so one man sharpens another.

PROVERBS 27:17

Perhaps you begin to build a new friendship and it is going well. But then you have a disagreement that proves difficult to resolve, and you both end up withdrawing into silence. Now you have a decision to make. Will you call that person and try to work out the conflict? Or will you let the friendship slowly die? You know it will be an extremely difficult and risky conversation; you know there is no guarantee that the other person will respond positively to your attempts to reconcile. You may not even be sure you want him or her to engage in the process.

If you pay the difficult price of relational integrity now, you may well receive a wonderful payoff in the future. So you make the telephone call. You say, "I know this is going to be a difficult conversation. But I think we have to talk. If we can face this painful issue and work through it, maybe we can re-establish our friendship and enjoy it for the rest of our lives. How about it?" It's hard, but the relational rewards will be worth it.

PRAY: *Do you have a friendship that is in conflict? Ask God for help in resolving the conflict, and for courage in initiating reconciliation.*

MONDAY

The Authentic Christian

Their delight is in the law of the LORD, and on his law they meditate day and night.
They are like trees planted by streams of water, which yield their
fruit in its season, and their leaves do not wither.

PSALM 1:2-3 NRSV

Authentic Christianity is not a set of doctrines. It is not simply humanitarian service to the less fortunate. It is a walk—a supernatural walk with a living, dynamic, communicating God. Thus the heart and soul of the Christian life is learning to hear God's voice and developing the courage to do what he tells us to do.

Authentic Christians are persons who stand apart from others, even other Christians, as though listening to a different drummer. Their character seems deeper, their ideas fresher, their spirit softer, their courage greater, their leadership stronger, their concerns wider, their compassion more genuine, their convictions more concrete. They are joyful in spite of difficult circumstances and show wisdom beyond their years.

Authentic Christians are full of surprises. You think you have them neatly boxed, but they turn out to be unpredictable. Over time, though, you realize that their unexpected ideas and actions can be trusted.

That's because authentic Christians have strong relationships with the Lord—relationships that are renewed every day.

PRAY: *Do you desire to live an authentic Christian life? Ask God to help you live this kind of life.*

An Authentic Marriage

Husbands, love your wives, just as Christ loved the church and gave himself up for her
to make her holy, cleansing her by the washing with water through the word.

EPHESIANS 5:25-26

Many marriages are superficial. Husbands and wives get all wrapped up in their careers. The kids' activities and needs dominate the limited time at home. And so spouses pass each other in the driveway. They sleep in the same bed and occasionally sit at the same table, but there's not much intimacy between them. They are cohabiting, but they are not nurturing one another. They are not involved in a vital, refreshing, authentic relationship.

Most couples settle for merely cohabiting. A few courageous couples, however, insist on more. Realizing it won't be easy, they nevertheless decide to fight for an authentic marriage. They know it will take time: they may have to give up activities that have been important to them. They know it may require some practical vehicle to help them make the change: setting a date night, taking evening walks, tossing out the TV, sitting at the table and talking to each other after dinner. They tear up their schedules if necessary and start from scratch, because the results are worth it.

APPLY: *What steps can you take to build an authentic marriage? If you are not married, what can you do to support other couples, or to prepare for future marriage?*

Other seed fell among thorns, which grew up with it and choked the plants. . . .
The seed that fell among thorns stands for those who hear,
but as they go on their way they are choked by life's worries,
riches and pleasures, and they do not mature.

LUKE 8:7, 14

Believers in Christ sometimes come to a point in their relationships with God when they realize they are no longer growing and maturing. Their walk with Jesus has slowed to a crawl or stopped altogether.

If this has happened to you, you may have to say, "That's it! I am not going to go through the motions of being a Christian anymore. I am not going to put my Christian life on autopilot, go through meaningless prayers and page through a Bible that I don't let saturate my life. I'm not going to play half-way games anymore. I'm going to pay whatever price it takes for an authentic walk with Jesus Christ."

JOURNAL: *Are you maturing in your relationship with God, or does your growth seem choked out by life's worries, riches and pleasures? Notice that both things we don't want (worries) and things we want (pleasures) can potentially squeeze God out of our lives.*

> *Then a great and powerful wind tore the mountains apart*
> *and shattered the rocks before the LORD, but the LORD was not in the wind.*
> *After the wind there was an earthquake, but the LORD was not in the earthquake.*
> *After the earthquake came a fire, but the LORD was not in the fire.*
> *And after the fire came a gentle whisper.*

1 KINGS 19:11-12

Listen to God. These moments in God's presence are the ones that really matter. This is where authentic Christianity emanates from—the unhurried, silent communing of God's Spirit with ours. You can't become an authentic Christian on a diet of constant activity, even if the activity is all church related. Ministry, Christian rock concerts, weekend conferences, church committee meetings— these all may be valuable, but they are not your main source of strength. Strength comes out of solitude. Decisions that change the entire course of your life usually come out of the holy of holies.

The archenemy of spiritual authenticity is busyness. It's time to slow down, reflect and listen.

APPLY: *How much time do you spend listening to God's still, small voice, compared with how much time you spend in Christian activities? Do you need to reduce the rpms of your life?*

Hectic Lives

> *Martha was distracted by all the preparations that had to be made. . . .*
> *"Martha, Martha," the Lord answered, "you are worried and upset about many things,*
> *but only one thing is needed. Mary has chosen what is better,*
> *and it will not be taken away from her."*
>
> LUKE 10:40-42

You don't have to be in business to be overcommitted. Women with small children know what it means to do ten thousand rpms all day long. Almost every minute of every day is consumed by those little creatures who pull on your pant legs, color on your walls, track mud on your carpet, throw food on your floor and then have the audacity to fuss in the middle of the night.

And it is incomprehensible to me how single parents can meet the incessant demands of work all day and then go home to face the even more incessant demands of their children, with no time out. I also see pastors, elders, church board members and others operating at a relentless pace.

Frightened, I ask myself, *When in our hectic lives do we allow the still, small voice of God to guide and correct and affirm? And if this doesn't happen, how can we lead truly authentic Christian lives?*

APPLY: *What pace do you live your life at? When do you slow down enough to hear God's still, small voice and allow it to guide you?*

Reflect on Your Life

My sins have overtaken me, and I cannot see.
They are more than the hairs of my head, and my heart fails within me.
Be pleased, O LORD, to save me; O LORD, come quickly to help me.

PSALM 40:12-13

If Christ's followers don't grow, it's because they do not make a habit of evaluating their lives. A few years ago, that was me. I was moving fast, always on the go but never looking deeply inside. And I was paying the price—committing the same stupid sins over and over, living with the same heavy load of guilt.

So I decided that each day I would try to honestly assess my soul's condition. I would look inside myself, and, with God's help, I would write down what I saw. Feeling awkward, I took out a spiral notebook and started to write. "God, here are some frustrations in my life. They aren't going away, so I might as well take a look at them." Or, "Here's a relationship I'm concerned about. It's not good, and I don't know how to improve it." Or, "Here are some blessings you've poured into my life." That embarrassing exercise was the beginning of some deep change.

JOURNAL: *Write some honest truths about your soul's condition. Ask God to help you to grow in the areas you've identified as problems.*

M O N D A Y

Speak Truth

> The LORD detests lying lips, but he delights in men who are truthful.

PROVERBS 12:22

Surveys cited in business magazines and management books confirm that the personal characteristic employees most value in their employers is honesty; above all, employees want to be dealt with truthfully. The same is true of employers. What they most want from their employees is the assurance that they can believe what their employees say and trust what they do.

When single people describe the perfect partner they dream of meeting and someday marrying, they inevitably say they want an honest man or woman who can be trusted in every way. They can't conceive of a marriage based on any other foundation than absolute trustworthiness.

Friends who have walked through life together for many years often name honesty as one of the keys to the success of their relationship. "We made a commitment to never lie to one another," they say, "and we never have." This is not just a formula for good relationships; it is what God expects of us. Why wouldn't we obey him when the benefits are so obvious?

JOURNAL: *Write about a time when someone was dishonest with you. How did it affect the relationship?*

A Lonely Pursuit

A scoundrel and villain, who goes about with a corrupt mouth . . .
who plots evil with deceit in his heart—he always stirs up dissension.
Therefore disaster will overtake him in an instant; he will suddenly be destroyed—without remedy.

PROVERBS 6:12, 14-15

Throughout the Bible we are called to the standard of truth telling, but nowhere more graphically and less diplomatically than in the book of Proverbs.

In an age and a culture in which lies and deceit are the common stuff of movies, books, talk shows, news reports and politics, the pursuit of honesty in personal life and relationships sometimes seems like a lonely and outdated endeavor.

God knew from the beginning of time that without a radical commitment to truth telling, marriages and families would disintegrate, friendships would explode, business dealings would fall apart, churches would be split by divisions, governments would become ineffective—the very fabric of relationships and society would unravel.

God calls us to a higher standard. The Ten Commandments include a prohibition against "giving a false witness against your neighbor." In other words, "Don't lie. Don't distort the truth. Don't use your words to play around with reality." Answering that call with our lives is how we build courageous faith.

APPLY: *To exhibit courageous faith in the area of truth telling, what changes would you have to make in your behavior?*

A Path of Destruction

The tongue that brings healing is a tree of life,
but a deceitful tongue crushes the spirit.

PROVERBS 15:4

God detests dishonesty so much because it destroys other people. How could a God who delights in loving and lifting up tolerate any act that "crushes the spirit"?

Every week at church I meet many people who have had their hearts broken by lies and deceit and twisted truths. "She promised to be faithful," sobs a devastated husband who has just learned that his wife wasn't. "He said he would never come home drunk again," cries a thirteen-year-old boy reeling yet again from the rages of his alcoholic father. On and on it goes—spirits crushed by dishonesty and deceit.

Do you remember the first time you were betrayed or lied to? The first time a confidence was broken or the truth twisted in order to hurt you? I'll bet you remember that experience in vivid detail. Did it make you want to stand up on a soapbox and shout at the top of your lungs: "Would everybody please stop lying! Would everybody please start telling the truth!"

JOURNAL: *Write about a time when you were less than honest. How did that affect you? the other person? Did your lies ever crush the spirit of someone else?*

THURSDAY *Dishonesty Disappoints*

The mouth of the righteous brings forth wisdom,
but a perverse tongue will be cut out.

PROVERBS 10:31

Many people lament that life is not working well for them. In many cases, if you trace their disappointment back far enough you discover a trail of dishonesty. It may have started with a slight departure from the point of absolute truthfulness, but all too often that first dishonest step leads to deeper forms of deceitfulness. Along the way, the dishonest person begins to experience the inevitable breakdown of his or her relationships with God and with others, whether in the home, at school, on the job site, in the neighborhood or at church. It's easy to place the blame on other people or on forces beyond one's control when the real cause of trouble is one's own careless or malicious mishandling of truth.

Have you told any lies lately? Any "harmless" little half-truths? "We'll do lunch sometime." Yeah, right. "I'll pay you back soon." Oh, sure. "Can I have just one minute of your time?" One minute? Really?

God promises that life works much better when we get off the trail of dishonesty and tell the truth, to him and to other people.

PRAY: *What comes out of your mouth: truth and wisdom, or lies and perversity? Pray a prayer of confession if necessary, and ask for God's help in telling the truth.*

FRIDAY

Do your best to present yourself to God as one approved,
a workman who does not need to be ashamed and who correctly handles the word of truth.

2 TIMOTHY 2:15

Do you remember how you felt the last time you lied? Most of us feel a little queasiness in our stomachs or a little heat on the back of our necks. You learn over time that lying is a messy business. It's always going to be, because we're created in the image of a truth-telling God. At the core of the character of God is an essence of purity that renders him incapable of dishonesty. Because of the piece of that purity that is at our own core, it will always feel unnatural and incongruous for us to lie. Think of the freedom that comes with truth.

JOURNAL: *Write about God's purity and about the fact that you were made in his image. How do you want to present yourself to the God whose image you bear?*

Stop Lying Now

You shall not give false testimony against your neighbor.

D E U T E R O N O M Y   5 : 2 0

If we trust the truth, there will always be warning bells and whistles going off in our minds, and that sick feeling in our stomachs. We weren't created to lie. The ninth commandment makes it clear: don't give false testimony. In other words, don't lie.

So the only reasonable choice for any of us is to stop lying. Now. Completely. If we have even the slightest tendency to distort the truth—and who among us doesn't?—we need to say, "From this day forward I purpose in my heart, with the help of God, to speak only the truth, always and in every situation, for the rest of my life." Such a commitment will inevitably improve our relationship with God and with everyone else. But we must be willing to draw a line in the sand and say, "Enough. No more half-truths. No more exaggeration. No more verbal twisting of reality. No more lies!" God will honor a faith-building decision like that one.

A P P L Y : *Whether lying is a big problem or just a temptation in your life, make a commitment to absolute truth. Notice what happens to your relationship with God and others as you live out this commitment.*

Spring

M O N D A Y *Fifty-Nine or Fewer*

> When words are many, sin is not absent,
> but he who holds his tongue is wise.

PROVERBS 10:19

Are we serious about truth telling? Then let's talk in practical terms. You want to sin less with your words? Then talk less.

Look at it this way. If you have three hundred conversations per week and you lie five times, your Liar Prediction Index would be three hundred to five. You want to lower the number of lies? Then watch this. If you have only two hundred conversations next week, you'll bring your net number of lies down to 3.3. Have sixty conversations the following week and you'll lie only once. And here's the real beauty of the system. If you want to stop lying altogether, have fifty-nine conversations or fewer.

You chuckle about this imaginary scenario, but I have found in my own life that the less I talk in a seven-day period the cleaner my conscience ends up being in regard to truth telling. The less I talk, the less I exaggerate. The less I talk, the less I say things I regret. The less I talk, the fewer promises I make that I can't keep. I suspect the same is true for you.

PRAY: *Ask God for his help on your journey from deceitfulness to truth telling. Ask him to help you to hold your tongue, to simply refrain from offering your opinion unless specifically asked.*

TUESDAY *Think Before Speaking*

The heart of the righteous weighs its answers,
but the mouth of the wicked gushes evil.

PROVERBS 15:28

At the end of the week, who will have made more progress toward becoming a truth-telling person—the one who carefully monitors her words or the gusher who lets whatever forms in his mind spew forth from his mouth? The Bible would vote for the person who slows down, considers carefully and holds back.

We don't have to participate in every conversation. We don't have to express every thought that comes to mind. We do have to pause and carefully consider our words before we speak. When ideas and words are forming in our brains, we should stop and ask: First, are our forthcoming words necessary? If they're not, why say them? Why needlessly increase the volume of our words and thereby create more opportunities for sin? Second, are our forthcoming words true? Are they absolutely, unquestionably true? If they're not, we should not spend one more minute thinking them, let alone speaking them. How many deceitful and destructive words might be silenced if we took the time to consider those two simple questions?

APPLY: *The next time you're tempted to jump into a conversation, ask the two questions mentioned above. Notice how often thinking before speaking causes you to simply fall silent.*

Will You Forgive Me?

Therefore confess your sins to each other and pray for each other
so that you may be healed. The prayer of a righteous man is powerful and effective.

JAMES 5:16

Anyone who is sincerely motivated to leave all patterns of dishonesty behind should heed this advice from James.

One of the best disciplines to which I have ever committed myself is the discipline of confessing any hint of dishonesty directly to the person most affected by it as soon as I am aware of it and then humbly asking forgiveness. Sometimes I am so blinded by my sin that I don't see it right away, but as soon as I see it I go to the person I have wronged. After asking for forgiveness, I tell the person that I am dedicated to becoming a truth teller, and I thank him or her for accepting my apology. If I respond to my sin of dishonesty any less directly than that, I end up forfeiting all sense of inner peace and joy. Without sincere confession of sin, I cannot get on with life and make it work.

Do you want to up your truth-telling average? Then invite yourself into the discipline of confession.

APPLY: *Decide today that every time you shade the truth or fail to live by your words, you will confess it to the person you have wronged.*

Keep Your Word

Whoever of you loves life and desires to see many good days,
keep your tongue from evil and your lips from speaking lies.
Turn from evil and do good; seek peace and pursue it.

PSALM 34:12-14

Don't assume that it is enough to confess only the flat-out lies and the intentional deceptions. What about when you say you'll show up and then you don't? Or you promise to be on time and then you arrive late? Or you agree to call someone and then you never get around to it? Is that an honest way to live? Does it allow people to build confidence in what you say?

Imagine how our families, schools, neighborhoods, work sites, communities and churches would change if everyone were committed to speaking only the truth in love. It can happen, but it has to start with you and me. We can't control anyone else's choice to speak truth or to tell lies. But we can make that choice for ourselves.

PRAY: *Ask God to help you keep your tongue from evil. Ask him to show you where you have let the truth slide, or simply not kept your word.*

F R I D A Y

When I kept silent, my bones wasted away through my groaning all day long. . . .
My strength was sapped as in the heat of summer.
Then I acknowledged my sin to you and did not cover up my iniquity . . .
and you forgave the guilt of my sin.

PSALM 32:3-5

If you sense a leading from the Holy Spirit regarding confession, you could begin now by confessing your sins of dishonesty to God. If you do, I believe you will sense from God a response something like this: "I know all about your lies, your exaggerations, your half-truths, your broken promises, your careless commitments. I listened and watched as you turned your back on me and yielded to every one of those temptations. But I love you anyway. No matter how far you have strayed, no matter how deeply you have allowed deceit to enter into your life, I still love you. If you're willing to turn from your sin, open your heart to me and trust in what Jesus my Son did for you on the cross, I'll forgive your sin, release you from guilt and gradually transform your life." Hearing this from God will strengthen our faith and inspire us to tell the truth in the first place.

APPLY: *What is God calling you to do? speak less? carefully consider your words? commit yourself to the daily discipline of confession?*

No Condemnation

Therefore, there is now no condemnation for those who are in Christ Jesus,
because through Christ Jesus the law of the Spirit of life
set me free from the law of sin and death.

ROMANS 8:1-2

If, as you pray a prayer of confession, you hear a voice inside that berates you, criticizes you and makes you feel worthless, that voice is not God. If you hear a voice that sweetly conveys how good you are and only brings to mind all the great things you've said and done, that is probably not God either. But if you hear a voice that expresses unconditional love, accepting you completely with all your strengths and weaknesses, being absolutely honest about your gifts but also about where you need to change, that is very likely God speaking to you. He is, you see, the One who offers us the priceless gift of truth and grace because he is the One who matchlessly combines these in his being. So we can listen to him with joy because he is honest, and we can listen to him with joy because he loves us as no other.

PRAY: *Spend some time confessing your sins to God, and then listen for his voice of forgiveness. Thank him that although he does not simply wink at our sin, he does indeed forgive us when we confess.*

M O N D A Y

If I have the gift of prophecy and can fathom all mysteries and all knowledge,
and if I have a faith that can move mountains,
but have not love, I am nothing.

1 CORINTHIANS 13:2

We tend to think of "love" as a free-floating feeling of benevolence toward all people. Often, it's a bit less glamorous.

On my way home from the gym one cold January night, I noticed a middle-aged woman in a dirty Toyota pulled off the road in a snow bank. I had things to do and people to see, not to mention wet hair, and no boots, hat or gloves. But I felt the convicting voice of the Holy Spirit saying "Love," and I reluctantly turned around.

The woman's trunk was cluttered. I had trouble finding the jack, and once I figured out how to work it, my freezing hands stuck to it. When I got the car off the ground, I discovered the woman had no lug wrench. Fortunately, she had a friend who lived only three blocks away. We were able to drive that far, where I finished the job in an unheated garage. The woman thanked me and drove away. Love is not always glamorous, but God asks us to love anyway.

APPLY: *What does it mean to show love to someone in need? Have you ever felt prompted by God to offer unselfish assistance? Did you do it?*

Love Costs

Therefore we do not lose heart.
Though outwardly we are wasting away, yet inwardly we are being renewed day by day.
For our light and momentary troubles are achieving for us
an eternal glory that far outweighs them all.

2 CORINTHIANS 4:16-17

I have found that love is a lot more closely related to work than to play. It has a lot more to do with being a servant than with being a hero. When I set about the task of loving, I usually end up giving instead of receiving. Love inevitably costs me something, usually the three commodities most precious to me—my time, my energy and my money. I do not easily part with these resources, because I have them in limited quantities. Tell me how to show love without spending time, energy or money and I will gladly sign up.

Tell me that love means sacrifice, however, and I become reluctant to commit myself. Maybe that is why some Christians emphasize the fun, fellowship and fulfillment aspects of Christianity without ever mentioning the sacrifice. It is high time to strip away the false glamour that the world—and sometimes the church—puts on loving. It's time to tell the truth: true love is sacrificial.

PRAY: *Ask God where he wants you to show love that is sacrificial, and then pray for the courage to do so.*

Ultimate Love

> *God so loved the world that he gave his one and only Son,*
> *that whoever believes in him shall not perish but have eternal life.*

JOHN 3:16

Because God was concerned with the well-being of people who were precious to him, he gave—he sacrificed—his only Son; and when you are concerned about the well-being of others, you usually have to sacrifice too. You may have to expend your time, your energy or your money for them. You may have to give up your plans, your independence or your privacy. To love as God loves, you may have to part with whatever is most precious to you for the sake of other people.

Sacrificial love is a difficult concept to grasp, because our culture teaches the exact opposite. We are constantly bombarded with books, articles, radio and TV shows, commercials and ads shouting, "You are number one. Take care of yourself. Don't let others steal your time. Save your energy so you can enjoy leisure moments. Stockpile financial resources so you can spend more on yourself. If you protect your time, conserve your energy and amass your resources, you will be happy." God calls us to be extremely countercultural, to love as he loves.

APPLY: *When you've made yourself number one, has it actually made you happier? What about when you made a sacrifice for someone else's sake? Which brought you closer to God?*

Mutual Love in Marriage

No one ever hated his own body, but he feeds and cares for it,
just as Christ does the church—for we are members of his body. . . .
Each one of you also must love his wife as he loves himself,
and the wife must respect her husband.

EPHESIANS 5:29-30, 33

My wife, Lynne, knows how to love sacrificially. One night I took her out to dinner, and she said to me, "I've been noticing that the demands on your life are increasing. Maybe I should quit writing and concentrate on making your life smoother."

Although I was tempted to say, "Great! And while you're at it, will you give me a backrub?" I held back, because I knew she was offering me one of her dearest treasures. "No," I said, "I really want you to develop your potential. Don't quit writing. Maybe I should say no to more things so you can continue to grow and flourish." And right there in the restaurant, we got into an argument—not the kind that destroys, but the kind that builds up.

Sacrificial love is the backbone of lasting marriages, even when it leads to impasses in restaurants. God calls us to love sacrificially, because he knows it ultimately strengthens us, and our relationships.

PRAY: *Pray for your marriage, paying attention not so much to changing your spouse, but to what God is calling you to sacrifice.*

Brothers and Sisters

Be imitators of God, therefore, as dearly loved children and live a life of love,
just as Christ loved us and gave himself up for us
as a fragrant offering and sacrifice to God.

EPHESIANS 5:1-2

The world does not understand the Christian concept of brotherhood and sisterhood. The world says to find friends among like-minded, like-incomed people who vote like you and have about the same golf handicap. These are safe people; they won't start asking for counseling or financial assistance.

These friendships work until you face a pressing problem, a tragic loss or a serious illness, and suddenly you realize that no one cares much about you.

Christian friendship is different. You find a few brothers and sisters and decide at the outset that you are going to expend yourself for them. You get into each other's lives. You encourage, counsel, challenge and rebuke each other. You make sacrifices. Some time ago, a close brother wrote me, "This letter is in part to tell you formally that whatever I have is yours. If you and your family ever need any kind of help, just say the word." That's a level of friendship some people will never experience or even understand. It's one of the joys of being a part of God's family.

APPLY: *Have you developed some deep Christian friendships? What steps could you take to initiate or deepen your most important relationships?*

Who Needs Love Most?

Jesus said, "It is not the healthy who need a doctor, but the sick.
But go and learn what this means: 'I desire mercy, not sacrifice.'
For I have not come to call the righteous, but sinners."

MATTHEW 9:12-13

My father always ended his letters to me with the phrase, "Love those people who need love the most." He put his words into practice in Kalamazoo, Michigan, where he helped a blind man start a restaurant, worked on providing safe shelter for vagrants in the downtown area and, when Vietnamese refugees flooded the country, adopted four or five families and found housing, cars and jobs for them. In addition to his heavy work responsibilities, every week for twenty-five years on Sunday afternoons my father led a hymn sing and Bible study for a hundred mentally retarded women at the state hospital. That is sacrificial love, and today's world desperately needs more of it.

PRAY: *Ask God to bring to mind someone at work or in your community who is in need of love. Pray for this person, and listen to God's leadings about how you can show love to him or her in a tangible way.*

MONDAY *Keeping God Out*

If I had cherished sin in my heart, the Lord would not have listened;
but God has surely listened. . . . Praise be to God,
who has not rejected my prayer or withheld his love from me!

PSALM 66:18-20

We aren't always willing to be broken by Jesus' radical love, because it takes courage to let go of our sinful ways and let him into our lives. Sometimes people say to me, "I sense that God wants greater control of my life, and I'm fighting him."

I usually tell them, "Don't worry—you'll win. You can keep God out. Slam the door, put bars on the windows and close your mind. You can stop him." But I also tell them that they don't understand who Jesus is. He knocks patiently until you open the door, and then he fills up your house with life's most precious commodities.

Christ is an altruistic lover: he loves us for what he can give us, not for what he can get from us. If you tear down the bars on your windows, unbolt your doors and fling them wide open so that he can come in, he will fill your spiritual house with everything it needs in order to be warm, beautiful and pleasant to live in.

APPLY: *Where are you fighting to keep God out of your life? What might you be missing out on?*

Not a Thief

> *The thief comes only to steal and kill and destroy;*
> *I have come that they may have life, and have it to the full.*
> *I am the good shepherd. The good shepherd lays down his life for the sheep.*

JOHN 10:10-11

Jesus is a great teacher. Knowing that most people think in pictures, he gives a picture of himself as a good shepherd. Realizing that most people have misconceptions about why he wants to come into their lives, he begins revealing his character by telling who he is not.

"I am not like a thief," Jesus says. A burglar's basic aim is to break into your house and find something of great value that will get good money on the market. You hardly ever hear of a thief who makes off with four dishtowels, two throw rugs and a tube of toothpaste; thieves look for jewelry, family heirlooms, paintings and electronic equipment. That's the character of a thief—to find what is precious and steal it. Jesus is the exact opposite of a thief. He does not come to rob but to give.

JOURNAL: *When you first encountered Jesus, what did you think he was like? A thief who wanted to take away all your "fun"? Someone who would focus on rules? At what point did your perceptions begin to change?*

Open the Door

Here I am! I stand at the door and knock.
If anyone hears my voice and opens the door, I will come in
and eat with him, and he with me.

REVELATION 3:20

Jesus is gentle, not pushy. He does not break into anyone's life; he stands at the door and knocks. If invited in, he wanders around the house placing precious objects on the mantels, on the shelves and in the cupboards. He fills up the person's life with everything life is worth living for: purpose, fulfillment, meaning, love, peace, confidence, security and even freedom.

A lot of people don't understand that about Jesus. They fear he wants to break into their lives and rob them of the joy of living. They are sure he wants to limit their freedom and make them live in confinement. They suspect he wants to take away fulfillment, put an end to adventure and stop the fun. If they had the courage to open the door, to get to know him, they would realize that their fears are based on falsehood. If we let him in, Jesus fills our lives with blessings and amazing, abundant freedom.

PRAY: *What, if anything, is keeping you from giving Jesus full access to your life? Pray a prayer of confession, if appropriate. If you have given Jesus full access to your life and are experiencing his blessings, pray a prayer of thanksgiving.*

Two Kinds of Shepherds

The hired hand is not the shepherd who owns the sheep.
So when he sees the wolf coming, he abandons the sheep and runs away. . . .
The man runs away because he is a hired hand and cares nothing for the sheep.

JOHN 10:12-13

Jesus, then, is a shepherd, not a thief. But there are two kinds of shepherds—owners and hired hands. A hireling makes a wage in exchange for doing what the owner asks. He tends to do whatever is necessary to earn his paycheck, but not a bit more. For a hireling, there is no emotion, no compassion, no fulfillment, no overtime and no extra mile.

While I was going to college, I was a hireling. I worked for a butcher, chopping up chickens. It was a job, but that was all. Sometimes the boss would say, "Bill, we're going to have a special sale tomorrow. Do you think you could stay a little later tonight?" I tried to answer politely, but inside I was thinking, *I don't care if this building burns down; I'm out of here at five o'clock.* That's the attitude of a hireling. Jesus is neither a thief nor a hireling. He's a shepherd who cares deeply for you.

PRAY: *What would your relationship with Jesus be like if he were only acting as a "hired hand"? Thank Jesus for the way he has been a shepherd in your life.*

A Caring Owner

But now, this is what the LORD says—he who created you,
O Jacob, he who formed you,
O Israel: "Fear not, for I have redeemed you;
I have summoned you by name; you are mine."

ISAIAH 43:1

Monday through Friday, business parking lots are always filled. On Saturday mornings, however, only one car is usually parked in front of each business—most likely the owner's car. Why? Because the business belongs to him. He wants to keep a close watch on the statistics, the cash flow, the deposits and the statements. He cares about it in a way his employees can never understand.

Jesus is a caring owner. We are his sheep, not someone else's, and he will walk miles to lead us to green pastures. Because he owns us and loves us, Jesus monitors every step we take. He knows every hurt we feel, every crushing disappointment we experience. We are precious to him, because he created us. He is in love with us, and he will do whatever it takes to keep us safe in his flock—he even laid down his life for our sakes. I'm grateful for a love like that.

APPLY: *Think about something that you own and care about. Your concern and care about that thing, no matter how important it feels to you, is only a fraction of the care and concern that God has for you.*

A Close Relationship

I am the good shepherd; I know my own and my own know me,
just as the Father knows me and I know the Father.
And I lay down my life for the sheep.

JOHN 10:14-15 NRSV

Because Jesus is our shepherd, we can become personal friends of his. Jesus says the relationship between us and our shepherd can be as close as the relationship between Jesus and his heavenly Father— what a mind-stretching thought!

To help us understand the depth of such a relationship, look at Romans 8:15: "For you did not receive a spirit that makes you a slave again to fear, but you received the Spirit of sonship ["adoption" KJV]. And by him we cry, 'Abba, Father.'"

Jesus does not want us to relate to him out of fear, as a slave relates to a master. Over a century has passed since the Emancipation Proclamation, and most of us have never belonged to a human master with total power over us, including the authority to injure us, kill us or break up our families. But we still have employers to relate to, and we still know what it means to be fearful. But our relationship with God is not based on fear, but deep friendship. What a promise.

PRAY: *Thank God for adopting you into his family, for offering you a close relationship with him, where you don't have to be afraid.*

MONDAY *In His Family Forever*

*How great is the love the Father has lavished on us,
that we should be called children of God! And that is what we are!*

1 JOHN 3:1

I once sat next to a person on a plane who worked for a well-known international conglomerate. This man said to me, "We do our work on a quota basis. If we come through with sales that meet or exceed the quotas, there's a future for us in the company. So far, for the eleven years I've been with the company, I've been able to do it. But they upped my quota last quarter, and I may not make it. That means my job is in jeopardy."

Eleven years of faithful work for the company and if he falls short of one quota, he's out! That employee could hardly miss the message—his value is tied to his performance; mistakes will not be tolerated. Jesus Christ says, "I want none of that. I don't want my people to be terrified slaves. I don't want them to think I love them because of what they can do for me. I love them for who they are—the adopted sons and daughters of God. And I want them to know they are in my family forever."

JOURNAL: *As a child of God, what blessings and reassurances do you have?
Write a note of thanks to God.*

Sons and Daughters of God

God sent his Son . . . to redeem those under law,
that we might receive the full rights of sons.
Because you are sons, God sent the Spirit of his Son into our hearts,
the Spirit who calls out, "Abba, Father."

GALATIANS 4:4-6

Years ago, Lynne and I took in an eight-year-old boy and a three-year-old girl who, because of their parents' alcoholism and divorce, had been passed from home to home. For several months they lived with us, and we grew to love them. The boy was just putting the finishing touches on a model car I'd bought him, when I had to tell him that the authorities were transferring him to another home. Tears came to his eyes, and then he got angry. He took his little fist and hit the model right on its top, shattering it into a million pieces. "I feel like a football," he said.

All human beings long for family permanence, but most of us quickly learn that it will not be found in an earthly family. Christ recognizes that need and meets us by adopting us into his family. He gives us his name: we are called Christians. He gives us his inheritance: life eternal.

APPLY: *Where have you sought a place to belong? Where have you been disappointed in that seeking? What does it mean to be adopted into God's family?*

We Are Chosen

> *He chose us in him before the creation of the world*
> *to be holy and blameless in his sight.*
> *In love he predestined us to be adopted as his sons through Jesus Christ.*

EPHESIANS 1 : 4 - 5

I know couples with hearts full of love who yearn to focus that love toward some little one, but no little one arrives. When these couples find children to adopt, they are absolutely thrilled. They don't warn the children that they had better come up to expectations if they want to remain with them. They don't tell them that they are allowed three mistakes, and then it's back to the agency. They accept them with open arms and joy-filled hearts because they love them, and they take them into their homes forever, give them the family name, and make them legal heirs. That is exactly how God acts when he adopts us into his family.

Just as a husband and wife who decide to give birth to or adopt a child begin to plan for that child long before it is born, God has arranged to take us into his family long before we realize our need for him. His love is radically inclusive.

PRAY: *Praise God for his inclusiveness, for his willingness to adopt not just you, but anyone who wants to be a part of his family. Thank him for specific things you enjoy about your relationship with him.*

Fellow Heirs with Christ

The Spirit himself testifies with our spirit that we are God's children.
Now if we are children, then we are heirs—heirs of God and co-heirs with Christ,
if indeed we share in his sufferings in order that we may also share in his glory.

ROMANS 8:16-17

Some people think of our adoption into Christ's family as a lovely metaphor that helps us understand the depths of God's love for us. This is true, but it does not go far enough. God has literally taken us into his family: the proof is that he offers us a share in the estate. Along with Christ, God's beloved Son, we will receive part of the inheritance!

However, when Christ came to earth on our behalf, he did not get any glory. The throngs cheered for him, but only when they mistakenly thought he was going to overthrow the Roman Empire. Everyone in Jerusalem knew he died like a common criminal; only a handful knew he was raised from the dead and ascended into heaven. This Jesus, who invites us to join him as brothers and sisters in God's family, also calls us to join him in obscurity and suffering. We do so joyfully, knowing that ultimately we will be rewarded.

APPLY: *How do you feel about receiving God's inheritance? What about his suffering? What steps do you need to take to build a more courageous faith?*

In His Family

> *Whoever does the will of my Father in heaven*
> *is my brother and sister and mother.*

MATTHEW 12:50

Jesus' comment about who was included in his family would have made perfect sense to his first-century listeners. They knew that you could not contest the patriarch's authority and still consider yourself part of the family. The Spirit's witness shows how Christ loves us—not as statistics in the heavenly census records, not as voices in the vast heavenly choir, but as individual, significant human beings. He does not want us to be timid or fearful, to live under the constant threat of condemnation. He wants us to be aware of the gift he has given us and secure in his love. He loves us as a brother would love us, because that is exactly who he is.

PRAY: *Spend some time thanking Jesus for his love for you, and the security that it brings to you. Ponder his love for you, aware that it is a gift. Express the love you feel for your heavenly Father.*

Join God's Family

I have set the LORD always before me.
Because he is at my right hand, I will not be shaken.

PSALM 16:8

The more I learn about Jesus Christ, the more I love him and realize he is worthy of my whole life's service. He wants to make me part of his family and give me the character qualities I need in order to live obediently, successfully and happily, now and forever. His heart overflows with love for me.

If you do not know this side of Jesus Christ, God longs to reveal it to you. All you need to do is say, "Lord, I am a sinner who could never earn entrance into your family. But because your perfect Son Jesus died for me, I am eligible for adoption. I want to be part of your family. Thank you for taking me in."

If you do that, God will take you into his family immediately, just as you are, and he will begin lovingly shaping you. He will send you the Holy Spirit and you will know that your status as God's child is legal, permanent and binding.

PRAY: *Today is not too soon to courageously say, "Yes, Lord, I want to be like Jesus. Please take me into your family and love me into your likeness."*

MONDAY

They Will Be My People

I will build them up and not tear them down;
I will plant them and not uproot them.
I will give them a heart to know me, that I am the LORD.
They will be my people, and I will be their God.

JEREMIAH 24:6-7

Throughout Scripture, we see this phrase over and over: "They will be my people, and I will be their God." A prevailing theme of God's Word is this idea of God longing and yearning to gather people into his family, into intimacy with himself. The story of the Bible is primarily about the great lengths God is willing to go to in order that we would be in his family.

God is saying to us, "My heart is so filled with love that I want to take you in and make you a permanent part of my family. Anybody—of any race, color, creed, background or hang-up—is welcome in my adoptive family." When we sincerely say, "Lord Jesus, I want to be a part of your family," the transaction is consummated and our adoption becomes legally binding and permanent. From then on, we no longer have the spirit of slavery. We are sons and daughters of God.

APPLY: *Have you become a member of God's family? If not, what is keeping you from accepting God's invitation? If you have, think of someone you could invite to join God's family.*

Two Are Better Than One

Two are better than one, because . . . if one falls down,
his friend can help him up. . . . Also, if two lie down together, they will keep warm.
But how can one keep warm alone? Though one may be overpowered,
two can defend themselves. A cord of three strands is not quickly broken.

ECCLESIASTES 4:9-12

When someone says to you, "Let's go for a walk," they're often using code language to invite you into the relational realm of life. It is another way of saying, "I'd like to open up my heart to you and have you open up your heart to me."

The passage above suggests that we all ought to build teams of people with whom we can walk through life—people who encourage us when we're discouraged, lighten our work load when it gets too heavy to bear alone, comfort us ("keep us warm"), and give us strength against the evil forces, temptations and trials we all face.

Many people carry fond memories of walks that proved to be significant in the development of a relationship. In some cases, a conflict was resolved; in others, a commitment was made or a bond established. Such walks are never forgotten.

PRAY: *Do you have a close friend who picks you up when you fall? If so, thank God for that person. If not, pray that God will open the doors for such a friendship.*

He who trusts in himself is a fool,
but he who walks in wisdom is kept safe.

PROVERBS 28:26

The book of Proverbs talks about relational walks, but not the kinds that last a few minutes or even a few hours. When Proverbs speaks of walking with friends, it refers to the kind of walks we enjoy with a handful of companions over the course of many years, sometimes even a lifetime. They provide not only friendship, but an opportunity to tap into a source of wisdom that will help us follow God.

Most of us have casual friends, acquaintances and work associates who pass in and out of our lives. But if we are fortunate, we will also develop a few close friends who become increasingly important to us as the years go by. Beyond our families, these people are the VIPs of our relational worlds. We socialize with them, recreate with them, enjoy deep fellowship with them and sometimes even vacation with them. In significant ways, our lives become intertwined. These friendships are essential to our spiritual health, because they not only bring us joy and wisdom, but they also draw us toward God.

JOURNAL: *Make a list of people who have been in your life for quite a while (friends, parents, family members) and who have influenced you in a positive way. Write a letter of thanks to God for providing these relationships.*

Walking and Talking

*These commandments that I give you today are to be
upon your hearts. Impress them on your children.
Talk about them when you sit at home and when you walk along the road.*

DEUTERONOMY 6:6-7

For many years Lynne, Shauna, Todd and I spent our summer vacations at our lake cottage in Michigan. Often in the early evenings we would sit and watch people walk along the water's edge. Sometimes we saw solitary walkers, but more often than not we watched people walking in pairs or clusters. Some would walk silently, but most seemed engaged in pleasant conversations. The same is true of the people I see strolling through city parks when I travel or the ones I see walking through my subdivision when I'm driving home from work. Walking and talking seem to go together quite naturally.

Many times I too have enjoyed the pleasure of walking and talking with family members and close friends, and I have learned that during these relational walks neither the exercise value of walking nor the destination of the walk is important. What is important is having the opportunity to share thoughts and feelings in a relaxed, unhurried manner with someone we want to be with.

APPLY: *Take a walk with friends or family. Talk about what God is doing in your lives, remind each other of his goodness and share ways to apply his wisdom to your life.*

Lifelong Partnership

> *Better a meal of vegetables where there is love*
> *than a fattened calf with hatred.*
>
> PROVERBS 15:17

While friends can be very helpful, marriage is an even more important relationship. In numerous passages the Bible makes it clear that God intends marriage to be a lifelong partnership. That is why the stakes are so high and why Proverbs uses such strong and colorful language to remind us of what it is like to be in an unhappy marriage. Anyone in a struggling marriage knows how painful it is to sit in a beautiful restaurant staring down at a juicy steak for which you have lost your appetite. Who feels like eating when the person with whom you are sharing the meal seems more like a stranger than a lover, and the distance between you seems more like a million miles than the width of a linen-draped table? Marriage is a relationship worth working on.

APPLY: *If you are married, spend some time thinking about that relationship. Is it as strong as it could be? If you are not married, think about your parents' marriage. What lessons can you learn from the strengths and weaknesses of their relationship?*

Take It Slow

> *A wife of noble character who can find? She is worth far more than rubies.*
> *Her husband has full confidence in her and lacks nothing of value.*

PROVERBS 31:10-11

A Kansas State University study showed a strong correlation between long courtships and satisfying marriages and between short courtships and heart-breaking marriages.

Rarely do couples caught up in the excitement of love want to hear about applying the test of time to their relationship. But they need to listen. They have everything to gain and almost nothing to lose by developing their relationship slowly. Every month of extended courtship either affirms or erodes their confidence in the health of their relationship.

Either way, it is a winning deal. If a couple discovers over time that the relationship is not all they thought it was, they have been saved from a disastrous decision. Better to discover the truth about a relationship before marriage, when breaking up is an honorable option rather than a violation of marriage vows. If, however, partners discover along the way that their earnest hopes about love and intimacy are being fulfilled in their mutual, growing relationship, they can move toward marriage with greater peace and confidence and joy.

APPLY: *If you are married, how long was your courtship? Do you wish you had taken more time to get to know your spouse? If you are dating, how do you feel about taking your time?*

MONDAY *Accessible Wisdom*

A sluggard does not plow in season;
so at harvest time he looks but finds nothing.

PROVERBS 20:4

The LORD abhors dishonest scales, but accurate weights are his delight.

PROVERBS 11:1

The book of Proverbs takes the ageless, priceless wisdom of God himself and makes it understandable and accessible to regular people like you and me. Comprehending its wisdom requires no seminary degree; the book contains few confusing theological terms. The most down-to-earth book in the Bible, Proverbs puts pertinent truths for everyday life on the bottom shelf where we can all reach them.

Few of the proverbs fit in the category of promises; instead they tell us how life works. One thing they make clear is that, generally speaking, people who are godly, moral, hardworking and wise will reap many rewards. How did the writers know this? They learned it from a lifetime of experience. They were fallible people like you and me who walked with God and pursued his wisdom, fouled up and learned a few hard-knock lessons, observed the successes and failures of others, and wrote down their discoveries in order to share them with others.

PRAY: *Are you looking for more wisdom in your life? Ask God to use the wisdom recorded in Proverbs to instruct you in growing in wisdom.*

Gaining Wisdom

Blessed is the man who finds wisdom . . .
for she is more profitable than silver and yields better returns than gold.
She is more precious than rubies; nothing you desire can compare with her.

PROVERBS 3:13-15

Those who earnestly seek wisdom will receive rewards that far exceed anything they can imagine. You think you want silver? Wisdom is better. You think you want gold? Wisdom is better. You think you want fame, fortune, achievement, power? Wisdom is better. Nothing you desire can compare with her!

Do you know any wise parents who exhibit sound judgment in how they raise their children? Do you know any fathers who know when to encourage and when to admonish, when to be tender and when to correct forcefully? Do you know any mothers who know when to give advice and when to just listen, when to teach and when to let life's consequences be their children's teacher? Now try to put a value on those wise insights: How much are they worth? How valuable are they to sons and daughters facing the challenges of the twenty-first century? Certainly wisdom is a gift to share with those we love.

JOURNAL: *Write a letter to God, asking him for wisdom to deal with a specific situation. As you write, jot down possible solution steps you might take to begin solving your problem. Of these, which reflect God's wisdom best?*

Parents and Children

Parents are the pride of their children.

PROVERBS 17:6

I know a lot of smart and hard-working people whose lives are filled with difficulties because they were raised by foolish parents who did not teach them how to make life work. I know many others who are living fulfilling and productive lives. Often they say, "I grew up in a home with a wise mom and dad." You can't put a price on the legacy of such parents. Children who grow up with that gift agree heartily with Proverbs 17:6.

Let's turn it around. How much value would a parent attach to having children who eventually walk in paths of wisdom, who know how to deal with conflict, who handle relationships maturely, who deal with money prudently? You can't put a price on that either. As we read in Proverbs 15:20, "A wise son brings joy to his father"—and to his mother. God's wisdom is essential if we hope to build a legacy of faith to give to our families.

PRAY: *Did you have wise parents? If so, spend some time thanking God for their teaching and influence on your life. Are you a parent? Pray that God will help you to be a wise parent, and ask him to help you raise your children to walk in wisdom.*

Work in Wisdom

Do you see a man skilled in his work?
He will serve before kings; he will not serve before obscure men.

PROVERBS 22:29

People who work wisely and skillfully over a long time will be esteemed highly by their peers and superiors, and they will be richly rewarded. Again, this is not a promise or a guarantee, but it is generally the way life works.

I can think of a number of people I know who have neither dazzling talents, stellar credentials nor charismatic personalities but who nonetheless have risen to places of strategic importance in the marketplace, in government, in academia, in the nonprofit sector and in the church. These people have gained responsibility and respect for one reason: they have handled themselves wisely over a long time. In their work and their relationships on the job, they have applied wisdom from the book of Proverbs—wisdom about taking initiative and developing discipline, wisdom about speaking the truth in love and managing anger and doing good to others. The foolish people around them who neglected these principles eventually fell by the wayside, but these wise people are still on the job—and still receiving honor and reward.

APPLY: *Whether your job is paid or unpaid, in the marketplace, the church or at home, set a goal to apply the wisdom of Proverbs to your work in the coming weeks.*

Don't Be Irresponsible

Therefore, my dear brothers, stand firm. Let nothing move you.
Always give yourselves fully to the work of the Lord,
because you know that your labor in the Lord is not in vain.

1 CORINTHIANS 15:58

I'm concerned that sometimes people are so heavenly minded that they are of little earthly use. What they try to pawn off as divine leading is really a very human form of irresponsibility. I once met such a heavenly minded pastor. He was shocked to learn how much time I spend preparing each message I give. Ordinarily I put in from ten to twenty hours reading, studying, praying and writing out three drafts of each sermon. This pastor exclaimed, "You go to all that trouble? I just walk into my pulpit and expect a miracle." I was tempted to ask him if his congregation saw his sermons as miracles.

Don't get me wrong. I've seen God work life-changing miracles in the pulpit—even my pulpit! But I think it's wrong for you to put your hands in your pockets and your brains in a drawer, jump off the pinnacle and expect God to catch you because you're already on the way down. That's not faith—it's foolishness. God is calling us to be responsible with the wisdom he's given us.

PRAY: *Have you ever tried to hide your irresponsibility behind a pretense of following God's leadings? Confess to God, where appropriate.*

Fools and Folly

The discerning heart seeks knowledge, but the mouth of a fool feeds on folly.

PROVERBS 15:14

The way of a fool seems right to him, but a wise man listens to advice.

PROVERBS 12:15

The writers of Proverbs say the opposite of wisdom is foolishness and the opposite of a wise person is a fool.

Today the word *fool* often means someone with low intelligence, but in biblical usage, fools may have a high IQ and a reputation for success. What makes them fools is that they ignore God's wisdom, preferring to follow the shifting dictates of the crowd or their own fallible opinions. While fools often consider themselves clever, their cleverness all too often leads to their ruin. Their penchant for distorting the truth, their lack of discernment and discipline, their unwillingness to exhibit self-control and their apparent delight in throwing caution to the wind put them on a path to disaster.

The Bible minces no words in exposing and denouncing both fools and their folly. Repeatedly it warns that the path of a fool is a downward spiral, that folly begets more folly and that the end is destruction. It takes courage to follow God's wisdom, rather than your own, but the results are worth it.

PRAY: *Following your own opinions is folly. Ask God for his help in following his wisdom, rather than that of yourself or your friends.*

MONDAY

Infantile Folly

> *Folly is bound up in the heart of a child,*
> *but the rod of discipline will drive it far from him.*

PROVERBS 22:15

I hate having to think of myself as a fool, but sometimes I am. Sometimes we all are. According to the Bible, human beings come into the world with a definite bent toward foolishness.

Think of a baby sitting in a sandbox. All a baby knows how to do is act on impulses, so what does he do when he feels a hunger pang? He grabs a fistful of sand and shoves it into his mouth. He doesn't ask himself if it is wise; he just grabs whatever allows him to satiate his hunger impulse as quickly as possible, no matter how foolish that option is.

I do not believe that the "rod of discipline" implies that we beat foolishness out of a child. The point is that foolishness must be methodically driven out of a child—step by step, month by month, year by year—and replaced by wisdom. That is the only way we can grow out of our infantile folly and become mature people who handle desires and impulses in a godly, constructive way.

APPLY: *When in your childhood did your own foolishness get you into trouble? What did your parents (or the consequences of your behavior) teach you? How can you pass those lessons along to children in your life?*

A Fountain of Life

> *Understanding is a fountain of life to those who have it,*
> *but folly brings punishment to fools.*

PROVERBS 16:22

If anything in the Bible has been proven true, it is that the foolish gratification of impulses will lead to a sick society. We see people gratifying their sexual impulses by engaging in promiscuous sex and committing acts of adultery; we see them acting out twisted desires for power through rape, child sexual abuse and domestic violence. We see people gratifying their desire to possess what isn't theirs through embezzlement, thievery, cheating in school and fraud. We see impulse buying, which leads to indebtedness and financial ruin. We see people making impulsive commitments they don't keep and wrecking relationships.

Proverbs says this is nothing but infantile folly and that it is time for those who behave like this to grow up and follow the path of wisdom. That path, the Bible promises, leads to abundant life.

PRAY: *Ask God to direct your thoughts, to guide you and help you to follow the path of wisdom in your relationships, your career and your financial life.*

Ethical Courage

Do not use dishonest standards when measuring. . . .
Use honest scales and honest weights.

LEVITICUS 19:35-36

How much courage must you summon to operate ethically in the marketplace? What kind of guts does it take to be honest? We don't want to offend customers, and so we say, "The shipment will be there Monday," when we know it won't leave the warehouse until Wednesday. We want people to think we are honest, and so we say, "I report all my income" when in reality we have a drawer full of unreported check stubs at home. April 15 is a great day to separate courageous people from cowards, because that is when moral courage hits us in the wallet.

How much is required to stick to a conviction when everyone at the office, at school or in the neighborhood says, "You're hopelessly idealistic, old-fashioned and a little bit strange—in fact, you're a religious fanatic"?

APPLY: *What would it take for you to be completely and totally ethical in the marketplace? Be honest about where you are perhaps cutting a few corners. Could you partner with a coworker or friend to keep one another accountable in this area?*

Facing Temptations

Can a man scoop fire into his lap without his clothes being burned?
Can a man walk on hot coals without his feet being scorched?

PROVERBS 6:27-28

Few people are strong enough to make morally heroic choices in the midst of powerful temptations. Most of us discover that our good judgment wavers when the pressure is on. We would all like to consider ourselves invulnerable to temptation and sin. But part of maturing is understanding and owning our vulnerabilities. When we do that, then we realize how important it is to make the critical decisions of our lives well in advance of the situations or circumstances that tend to tap into our fears, our weaknesses, our unmet needs or our impure desires. We each have an internal collection of these negative tendencies, and we each experience the external pulls and tugs of a morally bankrupt world. That means we will each struggle with our own unique set of vulnerabilities. But that does not mean we cannot live with integrity. Good judgment and godly behavior is possible, as long as we are disciplined enough to make important decisions in the light of day, when our thinking is clear.

PRAY: *Spend some time examining your own heart, and confess to God your negative tendencies, your impure desires. Receive his forgiveness and ask for his help in making good decisions.*

Wisdom and Discipline Are Precious

Choose my instruction instead of silver,
knowledge rather than choice gold,
for wisdom is more precious than rubies,
and nothing you desire can compare with her.

PROVERBS 8:10-11

Some time ago I was in a small airplane in horrible weather conditions. I watched as the pilot in command flew us through rain, wind shear, thunderstorms and hail and finally brought us to a safe landing. I have taken enough flight training to know that what enabled that pilot to bring us safely through a threatening situation was the discipline of hundreds of hours spent in training classes, flight simulators and check rides with aviation officials—all to keep his skills sharp. Without that, there is no way he could have performed flawlessly under such adverse conditions. Our safety that night was the direct result of his unwavering commitment to discipline. As a result, he had the knowledge and wisdom he needed to fly safely through the storm. Dare we call such discipline an enemy? Wise instruction and the discipline to apply it are indeed precious.

APPLY: *Do you have the knowledge and wisdom you need to make it through the storms of life with courage? What disciplines could you incorporate to gain wisdom?*

God Wants to Help

The fear of the LORD is the beginning of knowledge.

PROVERBS 1:7

Do you want to begin the process of acquiring something that is worth much more than gold? You start by obtaining the knowledge that is most central to the deepest human needs, the knowledge that there is a God who is powerful and personal and head over heels in love with each and every one of us, a God who has extended to us, though Jesus Christ his Son, the hand of forgiveness and grace. He says, "Come on, take that hand, and I'll help you make your life work." That is where we start.

Some people are tempted to say, "Okay, you're right. Enough folly. But I don't need God. I'm going on the self-improvement plan. I'll just start making better choices on my own." Such people are usually destined to make nearly the same choices in the future as they made in the past. They need to put their hand in God's hand in order to receive a new power to go a new way. And that new way leads to a life far better than anything we can construct on our own.

JOURNAL: *Write about a time in your life when you tried to make life work without God's help. What happened? Then write a letter to God asking him to help you make better choices in life.*

M O N D A Y *Minds Set on the Spirit*

*Those who live in accordance with the Spirit
have their minds set on what the Spirit desires. . . . [You are controlled] by the Spirit,
if the Spirit of God lives in you. And if anyone does not have the
Spirit of Christ, he does not belong to Christ.*

ROMANS 8:5, 9

One way God speaks to us is through people. "I provide for you," he says, as a neighbor shows up with a casserole we had no time to cook. "I care for you," he says, through the arms of a friend who seeks to console us. "I guide you," he says, through a counselor who points us to God's path.

Another way God speaks to us is through direct leadings of the Holy Spirit. This third Person of the Godhead is ready, willing and able to communicate with us. According to Scripture, he leads, rebukes, affirms, comforts and assures Christ's followers.

A lot of Christians, however, don't expect God to speak to them. By their actions you would expect that Jesus packed up and went back to heaven forty days after his resurrection and hasn't been heard from since. Though this attitude is common, it does not fit the picture of God painted throughout Scripture.

APPLY: *Do you believe and expect God's Spirit to speak to you? Have you ever experienced this? How does communication with God's Spirit help you build courageous faith?*

Spirit Poured Out

I will pour out my Spirit on all people.
Your sons and daughters will prophesy, your old men will dream dreams,
your young men will see visions. Even on my servants, both men and women,
I will pour out my Spirit in those days.

JOEL 2:28-29

According to the Bible, this ancient prophecy was fulfilled in the early church (see Acts 2) and is continuing even today.

God spoke to Saul the persecutor through a blinding light on the Damascus road. He then guided Paul the apostle as he traveled across the Roman Empire preaching the gospel. He spoke to the apostle Peter through a vision, telling him to extend Christian fellowship to a Gentile household. He spoke to the apostle John during his exile on a lonely island, showing him God's purposes in human history. Through the Holy Spirit, he guided all the members of the early church as they selected leaders, provided for each other's needs and carried the good news of Jesus Christ wherever they went.

And Jesus promised that the Holy Spirit would stay with the church—his followers—forever. He continues to guide and lead us. What a faith-building promise!

JOURNAL: *Write down two or three examples of times that the Spirit guided you as you made a decision. Thank God for his gift of the Holy Spirit.*

WEDNESDAY *God Still Speaks*

I will ask the Father, and he will give you another
Counselor to be with you forever—the Spirit of truth.
The world cannot accept him, because it neither sees him nor knows him.
But you know him, for he lives with you and will be in you.
I will not leave you as orphans; I will come to you.

JOHN 14:16-18

It makes no sense to believe that God lost his voice at the end of the first century. If the essence of Christianity is a personal relationship between the almighty God and individual human beings, it stands to reason that God still speaks to believers today. You can't build a relationship on one-way speeches. You need frequent, sustained, intimate contact between two persons, both of whom speak and both of whom listen.

A two-way conversation between a mortal human being and the infinite God would certainly be supernatural—but what's so surprising about that? The normal Christian life has a supernatural dimension. As the apostle Paul says in 2 Corinthians 5:7, "We live by faith, not by sight." If we listen, we can hear God's voice.

PRAY: *Spend some time reflecting on the Scripture above. Thank God for the promises in his Word.*

Live by the Spirit

So I say, live by the Spirit, and you will not gratify the desires of the sinful nature. . . .
Since we live by the Spirit, let us keep in step with the Spirit.

GALATIANS 5:16, 25

Listening to God speak to us through his Holy Spirit is not only normal; it is essential. Once a person turns his or her life over to Jesus Christ, it is no longer business as usual. Life no longer consists only of that which can be seen or smelled or felt or figured out by human logic. It includes walking by faith, and that means opening oneself to the miraculous ministry of the Holy Spirit.

And yet some of us are reluctant to open ourselves to God's leadings. We may know Christians who claim to be doing this, but their approach makes us uncomfortable. They have performed a kind of intellectual lobotomy on themselves, and they expect the Holy Spirit to choose their socks in the morning and their restaurant for dinner. They claim to experience a leading an hour, a vision a day, a miracle a week. Don't be intimidated by this approach. Learn to listen to God and walk by faith.

A P P L Y : *What does it men to be "led by the Spirit"? Maybe not having God choose your socks in the morning, but what decisions would you ask God to lead you through?*

The Spirit's Fire

Do not put out the Spirit's fire; do not treat prophecies with contempt.
Test everything. Hold on to the good.

1 THESSALONIANS 5:19-21

In reaction to obvious misinterpretations and abuses of the Holy Spirit's ministry, many Christians run in the opposite direction and become anti-supernaturalists.

To these modern rationalists, the Holy Spirit's promptings seem to go against human nature and conventional thought patterns. Accustomed to walking by sight, steering their own ships and making unilateral decisions, they are squeamish about letting the Holy Spirit begin his supernatural ministry in their lives. They wish the package were a little neater. They would like his ministry to be quantified and described. The Holy Spirit seems elusive and mysterious, and that unnerves them.

So when they sense a leading that might be from the Holy Spirit, they resist it. They analyze it and conclude, "It isn't logical; therefore, I won't pay attention to it." They question the Spirit's guidings, rebukes and attempts to comfort. But courageous faith demands that we use discernment, rather than just resisting things we don't yet understand.

APPLY: *What does it mean to "put out the Spirit's fire," or as the King James Version puts it, to "quench" the Spirit? Have you ever done this?*

God Wants to Speak

Let us then approach the throne of grace with confidence,
so that we may receive mercy and find grace to help us in our time of need.

HEBREWS 4:16

It's an honor to speak to God. We don't have to go through a priest or a saint or any other intermediary. We don't have to follow prescribed rituals or wait for an appointment. Anywhere, anytime, under any circumstances, we can talk, and he will listen.

It's ironic, though, that most of the time we think of prayer as talking to God, rarely stopping to wonder whether God might want to talk to us. But as I've studied prayer and prayed, I've sensed God saying, "If we enjoy a relationship, why are you doing all the talking? Let me get a word in somewhere!"

One way God speaks to us is through his Word. As we read it and meditate on it, he applies it to our lives. A familiar verse jumps off the page just when we need it. It seems to take on new meaning to fit our circumstances. The verse has not changed, but the Holy Spirit gives it to us when it will help us the most. Listening helps us appreciate this precious gift.

PRAY: *Read a Scripture passage slowly. Ask God to speak to you through his Word; then listen for his still, small voice.*

MONDAY *How Do You Respond?*

Jesus said, "No one can come to me unless the Father who sent me draws him. . . .
Everyone who listens to the Father and learns from him comes to me."

JOHN 6:44-45

Why is it important to be interested in the Holy Spirit's leadings in your life? Your eternal destiny is determined by how you respond to leadings from God. If you asked several seasoned believers how they came to personal faith in Christ, in almost every case they would mention an internal nudge that drove them into the arms of Christ.

"When I heard what Jesus Christ did for me," they might say, "I had a feeling, an inner tug to learn more, to walk a ways down that path to see what was at the end of it. It was like I was being led toward Christ."

Who draws us to Christ? God, in the person of the Holy Spirit, draws and loves and tugs seekers to the cross. If you're a Christian, you probably can remember the tug that led you first to the acknowledgment that Christ paid for your sin, and then to repentance, forgiveness and newness of life. The wonderful thing is, even after you're a Christian, God keeps tugging!

JOURNAL: *Write about the "internal nudge" that drove you into the arms of Christ. If God's Spirit spoke to you then, what's keeping you from hearing his voice now?*

The Spirit and Assurance

The Spirit himself testifies with our spirit that we are God's children.

ROMANS 8:16

In an airport, airline passengers with confirmed tickets read newspapers, chat with their friends or sleep. The ones on standby pace back and forth by the ticket counter. The difference is caused by the confidence factor.

If you knew that in fifteen minutes you would have to stand in judgment before the Holy God and learn your eternal destiny, what would your reaction be? Would you pace nervously? Would you say to yourself, *I don't know what God's going to say—will it be "Welcome home, child," or will it be "Depart from me; I never knew you"*?

Or would you drop to your knees and worship Jesus Christ? Would you say to yourself, *I just can't wait, because I know God is going to open the door and invite me in?* Again, the difference is caused by the confidence factor.

What does this have to do with leadings? The Holy Spirit whispers and makes impressions on the spirits of true believers, and this is what he says: "Rejoice! You've trusted Christ, and now you're a member of the family. Relax! The agonizing is over; you're on the flight to heaven."

A P P L Y : *When you think about your eternal destiny, do you feel like a passenger with a confirmed ticket or like someone on standby? What do you base those feelings on?*

The Spirit as a Witness

We know that we live in him and he in us,
because he has given us of his Spirit.

1 JOHN 4:13

In today's culture we thrive on legal documents. When you get married, you get a marriage license. When you buy a home, you get a title. When you buy a car, you get registration papers. In our adoption into God's family, the evidence God has given us is more important and more binding than any piece of paper—it is the daily and hourly announcement of the Holy Spirit to our own spirits that we belong to God.

God does not want us to wonder how we stand with him. I cannot always explain the inner witness of the Spirit or describe it, but I can testify that it is real. When people say to me, "I don't know if I'm a Christian or not. I hope I am," I get worried, because the Bible clearly states that when you give your heart to the Lord, he becomes real to you and you know you belong to him. The Holy Spirit lives inside you and repeatedly whispers, "Have confidence— you are part of God's family."

PRAY: *Do you ever wonder whether or not you are a Christian? If you have asked Jesus to be your forgiver and leader, you are! Talk to God about your doubts. Listen for his reassurance.*

"The word is near you; it is in your mouth and in your heart,"
that is, the word of faith we are proclaiming:
That if you confess with your mouth, "Jesus is Lord," and believe in your heart
that God raised him from the dead, you will be saved.

ROMANS 10:8-9

In a hundred different ways, using all kinds of leadings, the Holy Spirit comforts and communicates with believers, convincing them that they can have absolute confidence they are accepted into God's family.

That's the way to live—unafraid of death, because the Holy Spirit has assured you of where you will be beyond the grave. God promises that kind of assurance to his family members. If your experience is not like that, if you identify with the airport pacers, you probably haven't yet put your trust entirely in Christ. You may still be trying to earn your own ticket to heaven. Your anxiety can be your best friend, if it drives you into Christ's arms for assurance of God's love for you.

PRAY: *Do you know for sure that you are a child of God? What barriers stand in the way of your joining his family? Can you confess that Jesus is Lord? Do you believe God raised him from the dead? Spend some time praying about your relationship with him.*

The Spirit and Christian Growth

When he, the Spirit of truth, comes, he will guide you into all truth.

JOHN 16:13

Your growth as a Christian depends on receiving and responding to leadings. The Holy Spirit will prompt you and guide you as you read the Bible.

As believers, of course, we are responsible to obey God's entire Word. But the Bible is a big book, and we can't swallow it all at once. So God often gives us his truth one bite-sized piece at a time. This is what he did for me.

When I became a Christian at sixteen, I sensed the Holy Spirit saying, "You need to understand doctrine: the difference between grace and good works as a means of getting to heaven, the meaning of faith, the identity of God, the person of Jesus Christ, the work of the Holy Spirit." So I studied, prayed and took courses on doctrinal issues.

A few years later, the focus changed to my character. Every time I turned around the Holy Spirit seemed to say to me, "You need to grow in sensitivity and compassion."

APPLY: *What area is the Spirit working on in your life these days? If you're not sure, what could you do to pay better attention to the Spirit?*

The Spirit and Guidance

"For I know the plans I have for you," declares the LORD,
"plans to prosper you and not to harm you, plans to give you hope and a future."

JEREMIAH 29:11

You matter to God. He made you, and he knows what will fulfill you. He knows what vocation is best suited to your talents and abilities. He knows if you should marry or remain single, and if you marry, he knows which marriage partner is best suited to you. He knows what church you can flourish in. And this is what he says to you: "I want to guide your life. I know the path that will glorify me and be productive for you, and I want to put you on it. I'll do that primarily through leadings, so quiet your life and listen to me."

We ought to be attuned to the leadings of the Holy Spirit because our life plans are greatly affected by how we receive and respond to God's leadings.

PRAY: *Spend some time asking God to guide you, and to reveal his plans for you. Then take some time to listen to him. He may not reveal the whole journey of your life, but he will often guide you in the next step he wants you to take.*

MONDAY *Answers from God*

> *The LORD came and stood there, calling as at the others times,*
> *"Samuel! Samuel!" Then Samuel said, "Speak, for your servant is listening."*

1 SAMUEL 3:10

Suppose that you took some time to quiet your spirit before God and pray as Samuel did. In the solitude and stillness, what might God say to you?

To some seekers, God might say, "You've been reading Christian books and going to Christian meetings long enough. Now it's time you became a Christian. Come enter into a faith-oriented relationship with me." To those who have already made that commitment, he might say, "Return to me. It's been a long, dry summer. Let's get reacquainted!" To people facing trials, he might offer words of comfort: "I'm right here. I know your name, and I know your pain. I'm going to give you strength, so trust me." To others, faithful through hardships, he might say, "I'm glad you are being faithful even though life is difficult for you. Keep it up!" And to still others, this message might come: "Follow my leading and take a risk. Walk with me toward new horizons."

The message will be suited to the person's individual need, but the central truth is certain: we serve a God who has spoken in history and who wants to speak to us today.

PRAY: *Be silent before God. Then pray Samuel's prayer: "Speak, Lord, for your servant is listening."*

> *The LORD looks down from heaven on the sons of men*
> *to see if there are any who understand, any who seek God.*

PSALM 14:2

I know that God continues to speak to his people today, and I am convinced that there are two reasons we don't hear his voice more often. The most obvious reason is that we don't listen for it. We don't schedule times of stillness that make communication possible.

Be honest with yourself. When do you turn off the TV, the radio and the CD player, and listen to nothing louder than the refrigerator's hum? When do you turn off the soundtrack of your mind and come away from the numbers, machines, words, schemes or whatever it is that occupies your waking thoughts? When do you make yourself quiet and available to God? When do you formally invite him to speak to you?

Do you build the discipline of solitude right into your schedule? Try it! Like any new practice, it will feel awkward at first. Gradually it will become more natural, and eventually you will feel off balance if you don't make time for solitude every day.

JOURNAL: *Write out your weekly schedule. Then add solitude times, even if they are short, as if they were unbreakable appointments. Resolve to keep the appointments this week. See what happens to your relationship with God.*

Listen and Obey

> *Come, let us bow down in worship, let us kneel before the LORD our Maker; . . .*
> *Today, if you hear his voice, do not harden your hearts as you did at Meribah,*
> *as you did that day at Massah in the desert,*
> *where your fathers tested and tried me, though they had seen what I did.*

PSALM 95:6-9

One reason we may not hear God's voice is that we don't plan to do anything about it. God speaks; we listen and nod and say, "How interesting!" But if we don't follow up on the Holy Spirit's leadings, he may see no reason to continue speaking. People who make opportunities for the Holy Spirit to speak to them know that the Christian life is a continual adventure. It is full of surprises, thrills, challenges and mysteries. If you open your mind and heart to God's leadings, you will be amazed at what he will do. He is attempting to communicate with you more often than you know. You have no idea how much richer and fuller, how much more exciting and more effective your life will be once you make the decision to be still, to be aware and to obey God's leadings.

JOURNAL: *Write down any leadings you get from God during times of solitude. What happens to the frequency of such leadings when you obey them? What happens when you ignore them?*

Let the morning bring me word of your unfailing love. . . .
Show me the way I should go, for to you I lift up my soul. . . .
Teach me to do your will, for you are my God;
may your good Spirit lead me on level ground.

PSALM 143:8, 10

In addition to carving out blocks of time to listen to God, do you keep your ears tuned to him each day? A friend of mine has a company car equipped with a mobile communication unit that he monitors at a very low decibel level when he's in the car. Often we've been riding together, talking and listening to music, when all of a sudden he'll reach down, pick up the microphone and say, "I'm here, what's up?"

With all the other noise in the car, I never hear the mobile unit's signal. But he has tuned his ear to it. He is able to carry on a conversation and listen to music without ever losing his awareness that a call may come over that unit.

It is possible to develop a similar sensitivity to the Holy Spirit's still, small voice—to be aware throughout the day, even while going about your daily work, of God's gentle promptings. That's what it means to "live by the Spirit" (Galatians 5:16).

APPLY: *How can you increase your sensitivity to the Holy Spirit's still, small voice?*

Listening Requires Stillness

The people were amazed at his teaching,
because he taught them as one who had authority, not as the teachers of the law.

MARK 1:22

Very early in the morning, while it was still dark,
Jesus got up, left the house and went off to a solitary place, where he prayed.

MARK 1:35

People who are really interested in hearing from God must pay a price: they must discipline themselves to be still before God. This is not an easy task, but it is essential.

Jesus developed the discipline of stillness before God in spite of his extremely busy life. Crowds followed him wherever he went. Daily he preached and taught and healed. It was hard for him to find time alone to pray, and he had to get up long before dawn to do it.

Times of stillness and solitude were important to Jesus. In those times of seclusion, he not only poured out his heart to the Father, he earnestly listened to him as well. He needed his Father's comfort, direction, affirmation and assurance. Because of the continual leadings he received from the Father, there was purpose to his steps.

APPLY: *How often do you have times of solitude and stillness? Get out your calendar right now, and schedule some time alone with God.*

Delight in the Sabbath

If you call the Sabbath a delight and the LORD's holy day honorable,
and if you honor it by not going your own way and not doing as you please or speaking idle
words, then you will find your joy in the LORD.

ISAIAH 58:13-14

One purpose for the biblical command to honor the Sabbath day is that we all need time to rest from responsibilities and to receive spiritual and emotional nourishment. We need a weekly reminder that we are as accepted and loved by God when we sit quietly and restfully in his presence as we are when we are actively doing good for his sake. We need a weekly reminder that God is at work through our efforts in ways we can't yet see. We need a weekly reminder that we are just a small part in God's process of loving and redeeming his creation and that he doesn't expect us to haul the cares of his world on our frail shoulders. We need a weekly reminder that sometimes our earnest and faithful prayers are the greatest good works we can offer to others. To keep our bodies healthy, we need times of rest and recreation. To keep our souls thriving, we need spiritual rest and nourishment as well.

APPLY: *Do you keep a Sabbath, a day of rest? What barriers keep you from obeying God's command to give one day to him?*

MONDAY

Slow Down

> *Because so many people were coming and going that [the apostles]*
> *did not even have a chance to eat, [Jesus] said to them,*
> *"Come with me by yourselves to a quiet place and get some rest."*
> *So they went away by themselves in a boat to a solitary place.*

MARK 6:31-32

If we are involved in the marketplace, we are trained to believe that time is money. That's why we talk about managing time, using it efficiently and profitably, and—as a result of our concern—dealing with time pressures.

Cram more in. Start earlier. Work later. Take work home. Use a laptop on the commuter train. Phone clients while you drive. Check your e-mail while you fly. Schedule breakfasts, lunches and dinners for profit. Performance, performance, performance—it's the key to promotion, to compensation increase, to power.

Getting caught up in that intense pace can be rewarding! It's exciting when the adrenaline starts to flow and you get on a roll. But it leaves precious little time for quiet moments with God. In order to appreciate the rewards of time with God, we have to slow down just a bit.

APPLY: *Write out your daily schedule. What could you prune from it in order to slow down and have some quiet moments with God?*

Spiritual Journaling

God is our refuge and strength, an ever-present help in trouble. . . .
"Be still, and know that I am God."

PSALM 46:1, 10

If your life is rushing in many directions at once, you are incapable of the kind of deep, unhurried prayer vital to the Christian walk. Throughout this book, I've suggested topics to write about in your spiritual journal.

Journaling means keeping a journal—in this case, a spiritual journal. It involves writing down your experiences, observations and reflections; looking behind the events of the day for their hidden meanings; recording ideas as they come to you.

When I first came into contact with journaling, I had visions of people who would spend hours just letting their stream of consciousness flow all over endless reams of paper. *Not interested,* I thought to myself.

But over the years, I found myself drawn to the writings of a wide variety of people—mystics, Puritans, contemporary authors rich in their devotional handling of Scripture—who seemed to have one thing in common: most of them journaled.

In addition, I began to discover something about certain people in my church and around the country whose ministries and character I deeply respect. Most of them journal too.

P R A Y : *If journaling is something you avoid, and your life is very hurried, ask God for the courage to try this method of prayer.*

> *As the deer pants for streams of water, so my soul pants for you, O God.*
> *My soul thirsts for God, for the living God. When can I go and meet with God?*

PSALM 42:1-2

If you are not sure how to start journaling, read *Ordering Your Private World* by Gordon MacDonald. He suggests writing in a spiral notebook, but restricting yourself to one page each day. Begin by writing the word *yesterday*. Follow this with a paragraph or two recounting yesterday's events, sort of a postgame analysis.

Write whatever you want—perhaps a little description of the people you interacted with, your appointments, decisions, thoughts, feelings, high points, low points, frustrations, what you read in your Bible, what you were going to do and didn't. According to MacDonald, this exercise causes a tremendous step forward in spiritual development.

Most of us, the author said, live unexamined lives. We repeat the same errors day after day. We don't learn much from the decisions we make, whether they are good or bad. We don't know why we're here or where we're going. One benefit of journaling is to force us to examine our lives.

But an even greater benefit is that the very act of journaling starts to lower our rpms, so we can listen to God.

APPLY: *Does the psalm above express your desire to be with God? Try the exercise described in today's entry.*

Quiet Your Soul

> *But I have stilled and quieted my soul;*
> *like a weaned child with its mother . . . is my soul within me.*

PSALM 131:2

In the morning, once the adrenaline starts flowing, the phone starts ringing and the people start coming, I can easily stay at ten thousand rpms until I crash at night. So I decided to start journaling. What did I have to lose?

My first journal entry began, "Yesterday I said I hated the concept of journals and I had strong suspicions about anyone who has the time to journal, but if this is what it's going to take to slow me down so I can learn to talk and walk with Christ the way I should, I'll journal."

And I do. Every day! I don't think I've ever written anything profound in my journal, but then that's not the point. The amazing thing is, by the time I've finished a long paragraph recapping yesterday, my mind is off my responsibilities, I'm tuned in to what I'm doing and thinking, and my motor is slowed halfway down. If you have a desire for a deeper walk with Christ, how might journaling help you move toward that?

JOURNAL: *Begin with the word* yesterday *and write honestly about things that happened, how you feel about journaling, what you desire in your relationship with God.*

FRIDAY *Write Out Your Prayers*

If my people . . . will humble themselves and pray
and seek my face and turn from their wicked ways,
then will I hear from heaven and will forgive their sin and will heal their land.

2 CHRONICLES 7:14

Some people tell me they don't need to schedule regular time for prayer; they pray on the run. These people are kidding themselves. Just try building a marriage on the run. You can't build a relationship that way, with God or with another person. To get to know someone, you have to slow down and spend time together.

After I spend time journaling, I flip to the back of my notebook and write a prayer. To keep the exercise from overwhelming me and to ensure that I do it every day, I limit myself to one page. This takes a realistic amount of time, given the other responsibilities I face daily.

Once I write out the prayer, I kneel down and read the prayer aloud, adding other comments or concerns as I go through it. Doing this has strengthened my relationship with God tremendously, and it can do the same for you.

JOURNAL: *Try writing out your prayers, then reading them out loud to God. Is it easier to concentrate on your prayer when it's written down? What would it mean to humble yourself and pray in this way?*

Stillness Before God

I saw the Lord seated on a throne, high and exalted,
and the train of his robe filled the temple. . . . Then I heard the voice of the Lord saying,
"Whom shall I send? And who will go for us?"
And I said, "Here am I. Send me!"

ISAIAH 6:1, 8

The prophet Isaiah, before taking on an immensely difficult commission from God, listened to God in his temple. When he sat still, his vision of the Lord was amazing.

I used to try to pray and receive God's leadings on the run. But it exhausted me to be constantly doing and rarely reflecting on what I did. At the end of a day I would wonder if my work had any meaning at all.

So I developed my own disciplined approach to stillness before God that has made my life so much richer. After I've reflected on the previous day and written out my prayers, while my spirit is quiet and receptive, I write an *L* for "listen" on a piece of paper. Then I sit quietly and simply say, "Now, Lord, I invite you to speak to me by your Holy Spirit."

The moments with God that follow are the ones that really matter. This is where authentic, courageous Christianity comes from.

JOURNAL: *Write a prayer to God, and then write an L for "listen" in your journal, and sit quietly.*

MONDAY

Pestering God?

> *There was a widow [who kept pleading to a judge],*
> *"Grant me justice against my adversary." For some time he refused.*
> *But finally he said to himself, "Even though I don't fear God or care about men,*
> *yet because this widow keeps bothering me, I will see that she gets justice,*
> *so that she won't eventually wear me out with her coming!"*

LUKE 18:3-5

Many readers make a grave error in interpreting this story. They assume that we humans are like the widow. Impoverished, powerless, with no connections and no status, we are unable to handle our problems alone and feel that we have nowhere to turn.

God, then, must be like the judge, these misguided readers continue. He's not really interested in our situation. After all, he has a universe to run, angels to keep in harmony, harps to tune. It's best not to bother him.

If we're desperate, though, we can always do what the widow did: we can pester him. Bang on the doors of heaven. Ask our friends to pester him too. Sooner or later, we may wear him down and wrench a blessing from his tightly closed fist.

Does that interpretation sound right to you? I hope not. Please, please don't ever think of God that way!

JOURNAL: *List words describing how you think God feels when you pray. What does your list tell you about your relationship with God?*

Our Responsive God

Will not God bring about justice for his chosen ones,
who cry out to him day and night? Will he keep putting them off?
I tell you, he will see that they get justice, and quickly.

LUKE 18:7-8

According to Jesus, yesterday's story of the judge and the widow is not an allegory. Instead it is a parable—a short story with a puzzling aspect that forces listeners to think. This particular parable is a study in opposites.

First, we are not like the widow. In fact, we are totally opposite to her. She was poor, powerless, forgotten and abandoned. She had no relationship with the judge. For him, she was just one more item on his to-do list. But we are not abandoned; we are God's adopted sons and daughters, and we matter to him. So don't tiptoe into God's presence, trying to find the secret of attracting his attention. Just say, "Hello, Father," and know that he loves to hear your voice.

Second, our loving heavenly Father is nothing like the judge in Jesus' story! The judge was crooked, unrighteous, unfair, disrespectful, uncaring and preoccupied with personal matters. By contrast, our God is righteous and just, holy and tender, responsive and sympathetic. And he loves us deeply.

PRAY: *Confess any wrong view you've had of God, and ask God to help you know him as the loving, responsive Father he really is.*

WEDNESDAY *Abundant Blessings*

If you follow my decrees and are careful to obey my commands,
I will send you rain in its season, and the ground will yield its crops. . . .
I will grant peace in the land, and you will lie down and no one will make you afraid.

LEVITICUS 26:3-4, 6

When I bought my son a BMX bicycle, he thought *he* was excited—and he was! But after watching him ride it up and down the driveway that first day, I had tears in my eyes. I said to my wife, Lynne, "If that bike had cost five hundred dollars, it would have been worth it. I've never gotten more joy from giving a gift to anyone!" I got goose bumps watching him ride, seeing his eyes wide open with excitement. Right then and there I started making plans to buy him a Harley someday—and a car!

Just as I love to give gifts to my kids, we serve a God who is looking for opportunities to pour out his blessings on us. It's as if he were saying, "What good are my resources if I don't have anyone to share them with? Just give me a reasonable amount of cooperation, and I will pour out my blessings on you."

APPLY: *Give a gift to someone today—simply to express love—and notice how it feels. Remind yourself that God loves to bless you.*

Generous Fathers

Which of you, if his son asks for bread, will give him a stone?
Or if he asks for a fish, will give him a snake?
If you, then, though you are evil, know how to give good gifts to your children,
how much more will your Father in heaven give good gifts to those who ask him!

MATTHEW 7:9-11

When I was growing up, I had access to anything my father owned, just as soon as I was capable of handling it properly. One of his prized possessions was a forty-five-foot sailboat. When I was in eighth grade, my dad would say to me, "Why don't you get one of your buddies and take the boat out?" Once my brother and I had our driver's licenses, he was equally generous with the car. If he got a new car, the first thing he'd do when he came home was to give us each a set of keys and say, "Take it for a spin. If you want to take it out on a date, go ahead."

Most fathers love to be generous with their children. Jesus understood this, and that is why he used fathers to explain God's generosity.

JOURNAL: *Perhaps your earthly father was not always generous or trusting. But God is a generous Father. Make a list of good things God has given to you; then write him a note of thanks.*

The Spirit himself testifies with our spirit
that we are God's children.

ROMANS 8:16

My dad was a busy man who traveled all over the world. When he was in the office, it was hard to get past the switchboard and several secretaries. That's why he gave a few select business partners, his wife—and us kids—his private number. We knew that no matter how busy he was, we could call him anytime and be sure of reaching him.

I also have a private line that rings right on my desk. I've told my kids they can call me anytime for any reason. Believe me, no one's voice sounds sweeter to me than theirs. When I hear "Hi Dad," I don't care what I'm juggling. It can drop. My children are an absolute priority to me.

Now multiply a father's love exponentially, and you'll know how your heavenly Father feels about you. No one's voice sounds sweeter to God than yours. Nothing in the cosmos would keep him from directing his full attention to your requests.

APPLY: *Do you believe that God is willing to give his full attention to your requests? Is anything holding you back from praying to him right now?*

Your Personal Invitation

Let us then approach the throne of grace with confidence,
so that we may receive mercy and find grace to help us in our time of need.

HEBREWS 4:16

God is eager to pour his good gifts out upon us. Now we know that not only is he willing, he is also able to bless us beyond what we can imagine. But some of us are still hanging back, reluctant to crash uninvited into the presence of the King of the universe.

Hang back no longer! God, through Christ, has issued you a personal invitation to call on him anytime. In fact, it is impossible to come into his presence uninvited, because his Word tells us to "pray continually" (1 Thessalonians 5:17). As these verses tell us, you can pray about anything, and you don't need to be timid.

When you accept God's invitation, miracles begin to happen. You won't believe the changes that will occur in your life—in your marriage, your family, your career, your health, your ministry, your witnessing—once you are convinced in the core of your being that God is willing, that he is able and that he has invited you to come before his throne and do business in prayer.

PRAY: *Where have you been "hanging back" in prayer, not wanting to bother God? Spend time responding to his personal invitation to you; tell him what is on your heart.*

MONDAY *Develop Discipline*

He who ignores discipline comes to poverty and shame.

PROVERBS 13:18

When my children were young, I used to read them word association quizzes. I read the description of a person who worked in a particular profession, and the kids had to name the most important tool that person would use in his or her work. I'd read about a carpenter, and the kids would shout out "hammer." I'd read about a dentist, and they'd mumble "drill." For a surgeon, the word would be *scalpel.*

What was significant about each of these tools of the trade was that to the worker who used them, they were indispensable. Without a hammer, the carpenter couldn't build a house. Without a scalpel, the surgeon couldn't perform an operation.

When it comes to the work of living, Proverbs tells us that the most indispensable tool available to all of us is discipline. Without it, we cannot live productive, satisfying lives. While poverty and shame may manifest themselves in many forms, ignoring discipline always manifests itself in a life sliding toward ruin. If we fail to take discipline seriously, we do so at our own peril. God's given us a tool; our faith will grow if we use it.

JOURNAL: *Write about a time when you ignored discipline. What happened? What steps can you take to avoid allowing that to happen again?*

Discipline Is a Gift

The fear of the LORD is the beginning of knowledge,
but fools despise wisdom and discipline.

PROVERBS 1:7

The notion of discipline often conjures up negative images framed in punitive terms: we envision a child being spanked, a soldier being yelled at or a student being expelled. Or we think of discipline as an unavoidable evil, as an oppressive pattern of rigid routines and daily deprivations, imposed on us by some outside force determined to make our lives miserable. According to this view, discipline is the enemy, the obvious foe of a happy, meaningful, joy-filled life.

But not everyone views discipline that way. I recently read an article about a woman who wins many of the Chicago marathons in the wheelchair division. When asked how she manages to do well so consistently, she said that she disciplines herself to train one hundred miles each week. She sees this form of discipline as the only means of maintaining her competitive edge. It is the tool she uses to develop the strength and speed and endurance she wants to have. When she crosses the finish line, do you think she views the discipline that got her there as an unavoidable evil? Of course not! Discipline brings joy, meaning and success in reaching our goals.

PRAY: *Ask God to show you an area of your life that could be strengthened and made more satisfying by applying discipline.*

Therefore, my dear brothers, stand firm. Let nothing move you.
Always give yourselves fully to the work of the Lord,
because you know that your labor in the Lord is not in vain.

1 C O R I N T H I A N S 1 5 : 5 8

When I talked to a friend of mine before he had a major surgery, he assured me that there was nothing to worry about; the surgeon he had chosen had performed this procedure thirteen hundred times. In fact, he told me, people from all over the country wait weeks or even months to entrust themselves to this particular surgeon.

If we could ask that surgeon how he had built a national reputation for excellence and skill, I am sure he would describe to us years of studying late into the night, walking seemingly endless hospital rounds, examining hundreds of patients and doing routine procedures over and over again. If we asked what kept him going through it all, he might well answer with one word: *discipline.* If we asked him whether the discipline that kept him relentlessly pursuing his goals was a friend or a foe, I am confident that he would claim discipline as his dearest friend. Why? Because it has allowed him to achieve something of great significance that matters deeply to him.

P R A Y : *Talk to God about how you view discipline. Ask God to help you stand firm and give yourself fully to his work in your life.*

Aim High

> *Straining toward what is ahead, I press on toward the goal*
> *to win the prize for which God has called me heavenward in Christ Jesus.*

PHILIPPIANS 3 : 13 - 14

The first component of discipline is the establishment of a high goal. If this surprises you, ask yourself this question: Why develop discipline if we don't have a goal challenging enough to require discipline? Why pay the price if it is not necessary? If we are aiming for nothing more than a minimally challenging job, a few casual relationships or a passable spiritual life, there is little reason to develop or sharpen this tool of discipline. There is no need to bother with discipline if we can meander through life without it.

But if our goals are loftier than that, then discipline becomes a necessity. If we dream of fulfilling our highest potential educationally and vocationally, we need discipline. If we dream of being a spouse, a parent or a friend who breathes life into other people, if we dream of honoring God with our finances, if we dream of using our spiritual gifts in a meaningful way, if we dream of maintaining physical health through diet and exercise, we need discipline. High goals inspire us to live a disciplined, and more meaningful, life.

A P P L Y : *Do you have a goal in life that is challenging enough to require discipline? Do you need to adjust your goals?*

Growing Toward Goals

Hope deferred makes the heart sick, but a longing fulfilled is a tree of life.

PROVERBS 13:12

It takes tremendous effort to pursue dreams and reach goals. But what a payoff when we begin to see the fruits of our effort. A strong desire to grow comes from God. When we work hard and eventually fulfill that desire, we receive a reward that is energizing and beautiful, like a tree of life.

Throughout human history, popular thought has vacillated between the value of leisure versus labor. Current thought swings between the opposing views of those who so exalt the work ethic that they sacrifice nearly everything else to achieve their vocational goals and those who unapologetically flaunt their disdain of hard work and accomplishment. Can we avoid those two extremes and wholeheartedly agree that setting a broad range of high goals under the umbrella of God's guidance is a necessary step on the path toward a meaningful life?

JOURNAL: *Write down some of your life goals with regard to career, relationships and spiritual life. Are these goals high enough to move you along the path toward a meaningful life? Are they high enough to demand the development of discipline?*

Rewards of Discipline

*We continually remember before our God and Father your work produced by faith,
your labor prompted by love, and your endurance inspired by hope in our Lord Jesus Christ.*

1 THESSALONIANS 1:3

The payoff for spiritual discipline is a stable Christian life—maturity, useful-ness, satisfaction, contentedness. The payoff for relational discipline is a flour-ishing marriage and family life, along with a network of significant relation-ships. The payoff for physical discipline is a fit body, increased energy, resistance to sickness, lower insurance rates, higher concentration levels and increased self-worth. The payoff for financial discipline is freedom from debt and the satisfaction of knowing your little nest egg is growing.

The rewards of discipline are great, but they are seldom immediate. When the world clamors for instant gratification and easy solutions, it is hard to choose the way of discipline instead. But you will never build a walk with God, a marriage, a body or a bank account by obeying the world's law of instant gratification. Payday will come in its own time, if you endure the pain and put your nose to the grindstone now. Discipline will bring payoffs in whatever area of life you apply it.

PRAY: *Are you finding it hard to choose the way of discipline? Pray that God will give you strength and a long-term perspective to help you endure until you reap the rewards of discipline.*

Summer

M O N D A Y *Straitjacket Discipline*

> *It is for freedom that Christ has set us free.*
> *Stand firm, then, and do not let yourselves be burdened again by a yoke of slavery.*

GALATIANS 5:1

Do you take notes during talks and underline when you read; do you already practice a rigorous spiritual regimen? Before you dutifully lengthen your list of spiritual duties, back off. Do you need more habits—or more effective ones? Do you need to weigh yourself down further—or bring your heavy load to Jesus?

I fear that for too many believers, spiritual discipline turns into a straitjacket experience filled with requirements that squeeze the vitality and spontaneity and adventure right out of faith and life. For these people, Christ no longer brings freedom. Religion becomes a heavy burden. Most people can't live that way for long. Some of those who really work at it develop such a self-righteous attitude that everyone wishes they would fail.

JOURNAL: *Copy the Scripture above in your journal. Memorize it, and think about ways that you can be free in your relationship with God.*

Jesus' Well-Ordered Life

Then Levi held a great banquet for Jesus at his house,
and a large crowd of tax collectors and others were eating with them.
But the Pharisees and the teachers of the law who belonged to their sect complained
to his disciples, "Why do you eat and drink with tax collectors and 'sinners'?"

LUKE 5:29-30

When Jesus was on earth, he modeled a well-ordered life that was liberally sprinkled with mountain walks, seaside campfires, boat trips, wedding celebrations, slow-paced dinner parties and overnight visits with close friends. He knew he needed to be disciplined about the important issues of his life, but he also knew he needed plenty of room for the kinds of activities and encounters that would contribute to his experience of freedom, pleasure, light-heartedness and joy. So he arranged a lifestyle that honored that balance, and he invites us into a similar life of discipline and diligence, punctuated regularly with mini-celebrations that lift our spirits and make life sweet. I am seeking to emulate this kind of balance—and I love the effect it is having on my life. If we want to follow Jesus, we will emulate not only his more serious side, but his playful and joyful side as well.

P R A Y : *Ask God to show you what steps you need to take to balance discipline and diligence with freedom and fun. Then take those steps. Plan a party.*

Make Time for Celebration

The cheerful heart has a continual feast.

PROVERBS 15:15

If we intend to lead disciplined lives over the long haul, we need to integrate little celebrations into the pattern of our lives. One of the dangers of becoming a highly disciplined person is that it is possible to plan and structure the joy out of life. I know; I've been there. And I ultimately reached a point of joylessness that forced me to learn a whole new way of understanding God's comprehensive plan for a disciplined life.

God knows how he built us and what will contribute to our well-being. He knows that we cannot lead chaotic, scattered, unstructured, undisciplined lives and still experience fulfillment. So he invites us to well-ordered patterns of discipline that can put us on a path toward meaning and productivity and fulfillment.

But he also knows we need laughter and fellowship and fun and spontaneity and celebration; these provide a necessary, life-giving balance, so we don't inadvertently veer off the path of discipline and onto a deceptively similar detour that is legalistic, rigid, dull and draining. Don't go there! God calls us to celebrate and be joyful.

APPLY: *How often do you celebrate small things? What could you do to better balance order and structure with laughter and fun in your life?*

Enjoy God's Gifts

> Trust in the LORD and do good; dwell in the land and enjoy safe pasture.
> Delight yourself in the LORD and he will give you the desires of your heart.

PSALM 37:3-4

In addition to accepting the spiritual refreshments of the Sabbath rest, we need to give ourselves the freedom to enjoy God-given pleasures. We need to take the time to open our senses to the energizing beauty of nature or music or art. We need to let ourselves receive the gifts of good food, good friends or good books. We need to create time and space in our lives for whatever specific means God uses to refresh us, whether that be gardening or walking on the beach or sailing boats or painting pictures or running marathons. If our lives feel like constant drudgery, we are probably not listening to that whisper of the Spirit that calls us to rest and refresh ourselves. God has given us not just the option, but the command, to rest. Why would we ignore such a loving command?

APPLY: *How does God refresh you? What God-given pleasures do you need to create time and space in your life to enjoy?*

A Nonnegotiable Decision

Do you not know that in a race all the runners run, but only one gets the prize?
Run in such a way as to get the prize.
Everyone who competes in the games goes into strict training.
They do it to get a crown that will not last; but we do it to get a crown that will last forever.

1 CORINTHIANS 9:24-25

Perhaps you are thinking, *I don't need any structure or rigorous habits to make my heart grow. I go with the spiritual flow. I'm going to let go and let God do whatever he wants to do, and I'll just see what happens.*

This attitude, at best, is naive; at worst, it is self-deceived. We just cannot grow with no structure, no sense of intentionality about our spiritual life, any more than we can lower our body fat or develop good muscle tone or increase our net worth by just sitting back and waiting for whatever happens.

If a goal is really important to me, I discipline myself in order to achieve it. I decide in advance that practicing to meet the goal is nonnegotiable. Otherwise—count on it—I bail out at the last moment.

APPLY: *Which extreme (too structured or too undisciplined) do you lean toward? If appropriate, make a decision to become more disciplined in your spiritual life. Ask a friend to help you keep your commitment.*

Waiting for Your Call

*Do not be anxious about anything, but in everything, by prayer and petition,
with thanksgiving, present your requests to God.*

PHILIPPIANS 4:6

Whatever matters to you is a priority for God's attention. You don't have to pester him to get his attention. You don't have to spend hours on your knees to show him you really mean business. He's your Father; he wants to hear what you have to say. In fact, he's waiting for you to call.

If one of my kids called me and said, "Dad, please, I beg you, I petition you, I plead with you to listen to my humble request," I'd say, "Time out. I don't like the underlying assumption here. You don't have to go through all those gymnastics. What in my life is more important than you? What can I do for you?"

"Come into my presence," says God. "Talk to me. Share all your concerns. I'm keenly interested in you because I'm your Father. I'm able to help because all power in heaven and earth is mine. And I'm listening very closely, hoping I'll hear your voice."

APPLY: *Do you really believe that God is deeply interested in you? Realizing that you matter to him and that he wants to hear from you, what changes do you want to make in your relationship with God and the way you talk to him?*

M O N D A Y *Self-Deception*

The heart is deceitful above all things and beyond cure.
Who can understand it?

JEREMIAH 17:9

We have an enormous capacity for self-deception. Trouble comes our way, and our reflex reaction is, "God, what's up with this?"

I had a relative who smoked three packs of cigarettes every day from about age twelve. When he was in his early forties, he got lung cancer and started dying an awful death. I went to visit him in the hospital. His first words were, "How could God do this to me?"

A stockbroker loads up on high-risk dot-com stocks until the market drops. "Why did God devastate me financially?"

Let's not blame God here, all right? This is not about God. This is about you. This is about me. Owning our capacity for self-deception is the first step in solving our problems and growing in faith.

APPLY: *Think about a situation where you have blamed God for your problems or felt like he let you down. What part did you play in creating the problem? What steps can you take to remedy the situation?*

No Pity Parties

> *Why are you downcast, O my soul? Why so disturbed within me?*
> *Put your hope in God, for I will yet praise him, my Savior and my God.*

PSALM 42:5-6

The prevailing tendency is not to try to solve problems but to get stuck on them. A person is going along happily when suddenly he is hit with a big problem. His first reaction is to wonder, "Why me? Of all the billions of people on this planet, why did this problem hit me?"

It is not enough just to feel bad about the situation; he is soon calling his friends to bemoan his bad luck. He gets on his knees and tells God about the problem in vivid detail, as if God didn't know what was going on. He turns it over and over in his mind like a piece of meat on a rotisserie. Before he knows it, his whole life is revolving around his problem. Amazingly, he has done everything he can about his problem except the one thing he should do—devote himself to finding a solution to it. A courageous faith is one that looks for answers, rather than focusing on problems.

JOURNAL: *Write down a problem that is troubling you. Ask God to help you see your part in the problem and to help you find a solution. List steps that you plan to take to begin to solve this problem.*

All Things Are Possible

*Jesus said . . . "It is easier for a camel to go through the eye of a needle
than for a rich man to enter the kingdom of God."
When the disciples heard this, they were greatly astonished and asked,
"Who then can be saved?" Jesus looked at them and said,
"With man this is impossible, but with God all things are possible."*

MATTHEW 19:23-26

The disciples heard Jesus say that respectable, well-to-do, upstanding community leaders could not be saved. If that were true, then their chances of being saved were not very good either. They saw no solution; salvation was obviously out of reach.

Does your problem seem bigger than life, bigger than God himself? It isn't. God is infinitely bigger than any problem you ever had or will have, and every time you call a problem unsolvable, you mock God. "With God all things are possible." Visionary people face the same problems everyone else faces; but rather than get paralyzed by their problems, visionaries immediately commit themselves to finding a solution. They say, "The situation is bad, all right, but no problem is bigger than God. And right now, before I get bogged down, I need to start down the path of solving it."

APPLY: *Take one or two specific steps toward solving the problem you wrote about yesterday (perhaps initiate a difficult conversation, cut up your credit cards, ask someone's forgiveness).*

Divine Assistance

If any of you lacks wisdom, he should ask God,
who gives generously to all without finding fault, and it will be given to him.

JAMES 1:5

Like you, I have some mountain-sized problems that, humanly speaking, are unsolvable. But I don't want pity parties, and I don't want to get stuck on my problems. After reminding myself of the truth we looked at yesterday, I take another step toward a solution.

I go to a place where I can be all alone, and I spend some time thinking about the promise of divine assistance offered in James 1:5 (above). I force myself to believe that God will fulfill that promise in my case. If I cannot believe it right away, I pretend. I say to myself, "I'm going to act as if that promise is true." I say to God, "I'm going to take a walk, and I'll keep walking until I have some sense that you've heard my prayer for wisdom, until I know you're going to help me find a solution to this problem." Sometimes the walks are long, but eventually I believe. And as a result, my faith is strengthened.

PRAY: *Take a walk, and pray that God will hear your request for wisdom. Keep walking and praying until you get a sense that God has heard you.*

F R I D A Y *Solution~Oriented People*

Therefore encourage one another and build each other up,
just as in fact you are doing.

1 THESSALONIANS 5:11

When I am trying to deal with a problem, I pray about it and I listen to God, but I also listen to the people he's put in my life. To move toward solving a problem, I often meet with brothers and sisters in Christ who are solution-oriented people. I don't want to meet with people who will just sympathize. "Poor Bill, what a terrible problem he's facing." That does not help me much. It feels good for a while, but the next day I wake up and the problem is still there, big as life. So I meet with people who can tell me how they have solved similar problems in the past.

Once I've considered God's wisdom and the wisdom of others, I move forward in a spirit of humility, prayer and openness to the Holy Spirit. I trust God to close some doors and open others, unveil more possibilities or cause something to break in the situation until my problem is solved. Moving ahead, I end up thanking God for the people he's put in my life to build my faith.

A P P L Y : *Identify several friends who seem to be "solution-oriented." Arrange a meeting with one of them to help you explore ways to solve your problem.*

For God so loved the world that he gave his one and only Son,
that whoever believes in him shall not perish but have eternal life.

JOHN 3:16

The archetype of one who takes initiative is God himself. He created the heavens and the earth, spinning into motion the tiny sphere that is our planet. He lovingly spoke humankind into being, calling man and woman to name the animals he'd created, to tend to the garden sprawled at their feet and to live in loving community with one another.

But then he watched as man and woman disobeyed him and destroyed each other with hatred and lies and murder. He watched his creation spiral deeper and deeper into sin; he felt the searing pain as those made in his very image pulled away from him, breaking the bonds of love that had bound creature to Creator. How easy it would have been for him to yield to despair and to close his eyes to the ugly ruin his creation had become.

But what did he do? He responded with love and with a plan. He provided an option. He took the initiative in breaching the gap between himself and his wayward creation, sending his Son to reconcile us to himself.

JOURNAL: *Write a letter to God, thanking him for his love, and for taking the initiative and sending his Son to reconcile you to himself.*

MONDAY

Ask an Expert

> *One day Jesus was praying in a certain place.*
> *When he finished, one of his disciples said to him, "Lord, teach us to pray."*

LUKE 11:1

How can we learn the heart-building habits of prayer, the practices that expand our freedom and give us spiritual wings? According to a well-known business axiom, "If you want to know something, ask an expert." If you want to know about basketball, ask Michael Jordan. If you want to learn how to conduct an interview, ask Katie Couric. If you want to understand the computer business, ask Bill Gates.

It makes sense, then, if you want to learn good prayer habits, to ask the number-one expert—Jesus Christ himself. No one in history has ever understood prayer better than Jesus. No one has ever believed more strongly in the power of prayer, and no one has ever prayed as he did. His disciples recognized his expertise. When they stumbled upon him privately praying, they were so moved by his earnestness and intensity that one of them timidly asked, "Would you teach us to pray?" They knew that in comparison to their Master, they were mere neophytes—first graders in the school of prayer. Like the disciples, we can learn much about prayer by simply observing Jesus and heeding his instructions on prayer.

PRAY: *Ask Jesus to teach you to pray in a heart-building and life-changing way.*

 *Praying Like Jesus*

When you pray, do not be like the hypocrites,
for they love to pray standing in the synagogues and on the street corners to be seen by men.
I tell you the truth, they have received their reward in full.

MATTHEW 6:5

When the disciples asked Jesus for instruction on prayer, he simply assumed the disciples would have a regular time for prayer. He said "when," not "if."

That's a big assumption to make about Jesus' disciples today. Most of us say we just don't have time for daily prayer. But do we want prayer to become a vital part of our lives? If we want to develop in any other area—piano, basketball, physical fitness—we practice regularly. The America's Cup team from New Zealand practiced intensively for two years, six days a week, eight hours a day, and they brought sailing maneuvers to a level never before achieved. People who are serious about something always make room for it in their schedules.

If we want to live in God's presence, we need to tune in to God once a day, every day, without fail. We need to lay aside our other concerns and focus on God, look at him, talk with him, listen to him, sit quietly before him.

APPLY: *Schedule time with God each day for a week; strive to keep these appointments with God.*

Mean What You Say

When you pray, do not keep on babbling like pagans,
for they think they will be heard because of their many words.
Do not be like them, for your Father knows what you need before you ask him.

M A T T H E W   6 : 7 - 8

Be careful of clichés. How easy it is to use sanctified jargon while praying! Certain phrases sound so appropriate, so spiritual, so pious, that many people learn to string them together and call that prayer. They may not even think of the implications of what they are saying.

For example, I sometimes hear a mature Christian say very earnestly, "Dear Lord, please be with me as I go on this trip." When you first hear it, this request sounds holy. Unfortunately, it doesn't make sense. I'm often tempted to ask the one who is praying, "Why do you ask God to do what he is already doing?"

We don't need to ask God to be with us if we are members of his family. Instead, we need to pray that we will be aware of his presence, and confident because of it. Asking God to be with us when he is already there is one kind of "babbling."

P R A Y : *Do you find yourself asking God to do things like "be with" you? Thank God that he is indeed present in the situation you're facing, and pray that you would be deeply aware of that presence.*

Pray from the Heart

*In him and through faith in him we may approach
God with freedom and confidence.*

EPHESIANS 3:12

God wants us simply to talk to him as to a friend or father—authentically, reverently, personally, earnestly. I heard a man do this once when I least expected it.

I attended a conference with several high-level Christian leaders. The conversation was intense; I had to strain to keep up with the theological and philosophical discussion. At lunchtime, we all gathered at a nearby restaurant, the Hole in the Wall. A seminary professor was asked to pray. As we bowed our heads, I thought, *This prayer is going to sound like theology class.*

The theologian began to pray. "Father," he said, "I love being alive today. And I love sitting down with brothers in the Hole in the Wall, eating good food and talking about kingdom business. I know you're at this table, and I'm glad. I want to tell you in front of these brothers that I love you, and I'll do anything for you that you ask me to do."

His sincere prayer showed me how often I pray on automatic pilot. But God isn't interested in stock phrases. He's interested in authenticity.

JOURNAL: *Write a prayer letter to your heavenly Father. Write about the things that are on your mind and heart, in the type of language you would use in a letter to a trusted friend.*

Pray Specifically

Our Father in heaven, hallowed be your name,
your kingdom come, your will be done on earth as it is in heaven.
Give us today our daily bread. Forgive us our debts,
as we also have forgiven our debtors.

MATTHEW 6:9-12

Jesus counseled his disciples to pray specifically. He showed them what he meant by giving them a model prayer, the prayer we have come to call the Lord's Prayer. God-honoring prayers are not simply shopping lists. They are more than cries for help, strength, mercy and miracles. As Jesus shows by his model, authentic prayer should include worship and submission. Requests are certainly appropriate, as are confessions.

The Lord's Prayer is an excellent model, but it was never intended to be a magical incantation to get God's attention. Jesus didn't give this prayer as a paragraph to be recited; in fact, he had just warned against using repetitious phrases. Instead, he gave it as a pattern to suggest the variety of elements that should be included when we pray.

APPLY: *Spend some time reflecting on the way that you pray. Do you tend to be repetitive, or focus only on one aspect of prayer (such as requests for things you need or want)? Ask God to show you the truth about your prayer life and how it might need to change.*

Above All, Pray!

Be clear minded and self-controlled so that you can pray.

1 PETER 4:7

Whatever helpful disciplines you choose, practice praying Jesus' way. Make your prayers regular, private, sincere and specific.

Remember that God's prevailing power is released through prayer. He is interested in you and your needs. He is able to meet any need, and he has invited you to pray. His Son, Jesus, the expert on prayer, has given instructions so that you know just how to pray.

For the miracle of prayer to begin operating in our lives, we must finally do only one thing: we must pray. I can write about prayer, and you can read about it, and you can even lend this book to a friend. But sooner or later, we have to pray. Then, and only then, will we begin to live moment by moment in God's presence.

PRAY: *Spend some time praying in the way Jesus taught. If you feel there are barriers to the practice of prayer in your life, ask God to give you the courage to remove them.*

MONDAY *Ups and Downs*

> Be careful that you do not forget the LORD,
> who brought you out of Egypt, out of the land of slavery.
> Fear the LORD your God, serve him only and take your oaths in his name.

DEUTERONOMY 6:12-13

What causes ups and downs in our prayer life? Why do we lose interest in prayer? Why do we stop praying? One reason we let our prayer lives fade is that we are too comfortable.

If we don't have a difficult problem in front of us, we forget about God. It's human nature. When the storms rage, when the dreaded phone call comes in the middle of the night, when the doctor says it doesn't look good, or when your spouse says someone else is looking mighty attractive, prayer is almost second nature. In difficult situations like those, almost everyone prays—fervently, repeatedly, hopefully, even desperately. And then the storm passes, and God proves himself faithful yet one more time. A big part of our motivation to pray subsides, and the great prayer fade begins.

Understandably, this affects the heart of God. He is not beyond feeling used by his children. Especially when we act like college kids who phone home—collect—only when their money runs low. His heart breaks when his children forget about him.

APPLY: *Where is your prayer life right now? Decide today to talk to God in good times as well as bad.*

TUESDAY

When our fathers were in Egypt . . . from the hand of the enemy
[the LORD] redeemed them. . . . Then they believed his promises and sang his praise.
But they soon forgot what he had done and did not wait for his counsel.

PSALM 106:7-13

There is a sad theme running through the Old Testament. God blesses his children, and they forget him. He blesses them again, and they forget him again. They get in big trouble and beg for help, and God comes through with an eleventh-hour rescue. Yet they forget him once again.

Read, for example, the sad litany in Psalm 78. Though God gave Israel the law, divided the sea so they could pass through, guided them through the desert, gave them miraculous food and water, and drove back their enemies, "again and again they put God to the test; . . . they did not remember his power" (vv. 41-42). The same pattern is evident in the psalm above.

We don't want to forget God. We want our prayer lives to be consistent. How can we stay mindful of God's goodness? How can we remember to pray? It is only with God's help that we can be faithful to him.

JOURNAL: *Write your own psalm, listing the many things God has done for you.*
Use it as a reminder of God and his kindness to you.

A Daily Rhythm

Crowds of people came to hear him and to be healed of their sicknesses.
But Jesus often withdrew to lonely places and prayed.

LUKE 5:15-16

We can remember to pray the same way we remember anything else that matters to us—by scheduling it. Jesus always made time for prayer. If we find we are praying less and less, it may be because we have never made prayer a fixed part of our everyday routine.

Some people have a prayer time even before they kick off the covers in the morning. Others pray over coffee, or at lunch, or right after work or school, or just before bedtime. The time of day we choose for prayer doesn't matter, so long as we keep it faithfully. Prayer needs to be part of the rhythm of our daily lives.

Choose a time when you are usually undisturbed, when you can shut the world out and tune in to God. At the same time, choose a place that can be your refuge, your sanctuary, while you are sitting in God's presence. Setting apart a time and place to be with God will deepen your relationship with him and help your faith to grow.

APPLY: *Schedule appointments with God for each day of the next week. See how consistent you are in keeping the appointments. Try to grow in consistency each week.*

A Sacred Place

> *Very early in the morning, while it was still dark, Jesus got up, left the house*
> *and went off to a solitary place, where he prayed.*

MARK 1:35

The people I know who pray fervently and joyfully and consistently can usually describe the physical environment in which they pray daily. I know a man who prays on the commuter train five days a week. He gets on at the Palatine station and prays all the way into Chicago. That's forty minutes if he catches the express, and one hour otherwise. He says his seat on the train is a holy place for him.

Jesus often prayed outdoors, in solitary places. We can follow that example. I know someone who prays in the corner booth of a restaurant before work every day, someone who prays while sitting by a sliding-glass door overlooking a garden, someone who writes out her prayers on the computer in her home office. Any place can become a place of prayer. What is important, if we want to remember to pray, is to establish a particular place and a particular time for our meetings with the Lord.

APPLY: *Do you have a place where you go to pray? Today find a place where you can go consistently to pray and be alone with God.*

Eliminate Distractions

*Because so many people were coming and going that [the disciples]
did not even have a chance to eat, [Jesus] said to them,
"Come with me by yourselves to a quiet place and get some rest."
So they went away by themselves in a boat to a solitary place.*

MARK 6:31-32

Prayer, Jesus says, is not a spectator sport. It is not something we are to en-gage in to give off signals of spirituality. When you pray, go into your room and shut the door. Find a closet, an empty office, some secret place away from peo-ple and alone with God. That's where you can pray most effectively.

Why the emphasis on privacy? A private place ensures a minimum of dis-tractions, and most people find distractions deadly when it comes to making a connection with God. Almost any kind of noise—voices, music, a ringing phone, kids, dogs, birds—can cause me to lose my concentration during a time of prayer. Even a ticking clock can catch me up in its rhythm until I'm tapping my foot and singing a country song to its beat. Jesus knows how our minds are put together, and he counsels, "Don't bother fighting distractions, because you'll lose. Avoid them. Find a quiet place where you can pray with-out interruption."

APPLY: *Find a place in your home that can be your prayer place. Spend time praying there each day.*

The Place God Meets You

When you pray, go into your room, close the door and pray to your Father, who is unseen.
Then your Father, who sees what is done in secret, will reward you.

MATTHEW 6:6

When you create a secret place where you can really pray, over time you will look forward to going there. You will grow to love the aura of the place where you freely converse with God.

I created such a prayer room in a corner of my former office. In my prayer place I put an open Bible, a sign that says "God is able," a crown of thorns to remind me of the suffering Savior, and a shepherd's staff that I often hold up while making requests.

That office corner became a holy place. There I communed with the Lord. I poured out my heart to him, worshiped him, prayed for my congregation and received remarkable answers to prayer.

My office has since been relocated, and I now have a new prayer corner. But I have warm memories of the old one—not because there is anything holy about the corner itself but because of what happened there. Every morning I met with the Lord, and he faithfully met with me. Thinking of that corner is like thinking of home.

JOURNAL: *Write down your memories of a time where have you sensed that God was with you in a sacred place.*

MONDAY

Mountain-Moving Prayer

Jesus replied, "I tell you the truth, if you have faith and do not doubt, . . .
you can say to this mountain, 'Go, throw yourself into the sea,' and it will be done.
If you believe, you will receive whatever you ask for in prayer."

MATTHEW 21:21-22

According to the Bible, believers can be confident that their prayers will be answered. Our prayers are more than wishes, hopes or feeble aspirations—but only if we pray with believing, faith-filled hearts. That is the kind of prayer that moves mountains.

Jesus, of course, was not in the excavation business. He had little interest in relocating piles of rocks in the ocean's depths. He was using the term *mountain* figuratively. Whatever mountain stands in your path, whatever obstacle blocks your way, whatever difficulty immobilizes you, the prayer of faith can remove it.

PRAY: *Ask God to show you how to develop confidence that removes roadblocks. Ask for his help in learning more about praying with a faith-filled heart.*

Look at God

In the morning, O LORD, you hear my voice; in the morning
I lay my requests before you and wait in expectation.

PSALM 5:3

Faith comes from looking at God, not at the mountain.

An Indian leader in southern India has ministered with more courage and faith than most people will ever dream of mustering. His father, a dynamic leader, had started the mission in a Hindu-dominated area.

One day a Hindu leader came to the father and asked for prayer. Eagerly, he took him into a private room, knelt down with him, closed his eyes and began to pray. While he was praying, the Hindu man reached into his robe, pulled out a knife and stabbed him repeatedly. The son, hearing his father's screams, ran to help him. He held his wounded father in his arms. Three days later, his father died. On his deathbed he said to his son, "Please tell that man that he is forgiven. Care for your mother and carry on this ministry. Do whatever it takes to win people to Christ."

For over twenty years, he has been working with unbelievable intensity. He has started over a hundred churches and a medical clinic, all along looking at God, not the mountain.

APPLY: *What mountains stand in your way? How much time do you spend focusing on the mountain? Spend some time today looking at God instead, and pray accordingly.*

Take That First Step

The LORD said . . . "Tell the priests who carry the ark of the covenant:
'When you reach the edge of the Jordan's waters, go and stand in the river.'"
Joshua said . . . "And as soon as the priests . . . set foot in the Jordan,
its waters flowing downstream will be cut off and stand up in a heap."

JOSHUA 3:7-9, 13

Having spent their entire adult lives in the wilderness, this is probably the first river the priests have ever seen close up, and the Jordan doesn't look particularly friendly during flood season. And with a few hundred thousand anxious Israelites at their heels, it will be hard to change their minds and turn around.

Still, the priests had faith enough to obey, and when they did, "the water from upstream stopped flowing" and the entire nation crossed over on dry ground (Joshua 3:15-17).

God didn't give proof or even evidence that the waters would part. He did nothing until they put their feet in the water, taking the first step of commitment and obedience. Only then did he stop the flow of the river. In the same way, mountain-moving faith will be given to us as we step out and follow the Lord's direction.

PRAY: *Ask God to show you where you need to take a step of faith "into the river," trusting him to act. Then pray for the courage to just do it.*

THURSDAY *Move Over, Mountain*

Those who trust in the LORD are like Mount Zion,
which cannot be shaken but endures forever.

PSALM 125:1

How do you pray a prayer so filled with faith that it can move a mountain? By shifting the focus from the size of your mountain to the sufficiency of the mountain mover, and by stepping forward in obedience.

When the Israelites reach the Promised Land, twelve spies go out to survey it. Ten come back saying, "You wouldn't believe the size of the cities, the armies, the giants. We'd better look somewhere else." Two come back saying, "The God who is faithful promised he would give us the land, so let's go in his strength." Ten looked at the size of the mountain and fell back; only two looked at the sufficiency of the mountain mover and wanted to move forward. (See Numbers 13.)

Probably everyone is standing in the shadow of at least one mountain that just will not move: a destructive habit, a character flaw, an impossible marriage or work situation, a financial problem, a physical disability. What is your immovable mountain? Have you stood in its shadow for so long that you've grown accustomed to the darkness?

PRAY: *Shift the focus of your prayers from describing your mountain to the Lord to focusing on him, the mountain mover. Then follow his lead in faith, and watch that mountain step aside.*

Thimble or Barrel?

Let us acknowledge the LORD. . . . As surely as the sun rises, he will appear;
he will come to us like the winter rains, like the spring rains that water the earth.

HOSEA 6:3

In 1978 I traveled to Korea to visit the world's largest church. At that time, every Friday night from eight o'clock until seven o'clock Saturday morning, ten thousand people gathered in an auditorium and prayed that God would take the church's ministry by storm. Every Saturday, several thousand people went to a mountain they call Prayer Mountain, and prayed that God would work in a supernatural way.

In 1978 the church had 100,000 members. Some people might have thought it was large enough, but its members had a vision. Ten prayer-filled years later, the church membership was up to 450,000. Today there are over one million members. When we work, *we* work; when we pray, *God* works!

I've heard it said that if you bring a thimble to God, he'll fill it. If you bring a bucket to God, he'll fill that. If you bring a five-hundred-gallon barrel to God, he'll fill that too. Are you expecting God to fill your needs? Are you asking him to do so—regularly, earnestly, persistently? He promises he will answer—and your faith will grow as a result.

APPLY: *Where in your life are you coming to God with a thimble? Come to God often, expecting great things.*

Everything but Prayer

You do not have, because you do not ask God.

JAMES 4:2

How often does this happen? You tell a friend that you'll pray about something, and you almost do. But even though you think about it from time to time, you hardly pray about it at all. Why isn't God answering your prayer? Because you haven't yet prayed purposefully, fervently or expectantly. The most common cause of unanswered prayer is prayerlessness.

People often tell me how they have attempted to address a pressing need. They have gone to counselors, read self-help books, claimed biblical promises, practiced self-discipline, confided in Christian friends, practiced assertiveness or submission or self-denial or positive thinking, even read books about prayer—and their need is still not met.

I say to these people, "Look me right in the eye and tell me if you've prayed about this fervently and regularly over an extended period of time." Usually they shift from one foot to another, look down and mumble, "Well, uh, you know, uh, I guess not."

I understand all too well. Admittedly, I'm often a member of the club whose motto is "When all else fails, pray." God wants us to make prayer our first response to any need.

PRAY: *Identify a pressing need in your life. Commit to praying for this need every day for the next thirty days. Ask God to help you remain steadfast in your prayers.*

M O N D A Y *Contaminated Prayer*

> *Your iniquities have separated you from your God;*
> *your sins have hidden his face from you, so that he will not hear.*

ISAIAH 59:2

> *What does the LORD require of you?*
> *To act justly and to love mercy and to walk humbly with your God.*

MICAH 6:8

Unanswered prayer can be a result of unconfessed sin, which cuts off our communication with the Father. Sin has a way of contaminating your prayers, and keeping your Christian life from achieving its full potential.

God expects us to maintain strict personal integrity. He expects us to show thoughtfulness and love toward others and to maintain a relationship with him. If we refuse to do these things, we are presumptuous to expect God to answer our prayers.

If you're tolerating sin in your life, don't waste your breath praying unless it's a prayer of confession. Receive the Lord's forgiveness, and then he will listen when you pour out your heart to him.

PRAY: *What sin needs to be confessed? Are you aware of how it has separated you from God? Spend some time asking for and fully receiving God's forgiveness.*

Search me, O God, and know my heart; test me and know my anxious thoughts.
See if there is any offensive way in me, and lead me in the way everlasting.

PSALM 139:23-24

Some of us may no longer be eager to pray. Something we have done—or are currently doing—may be standing between us and God. Sometimes when I'm trying to help people understand why they don't pray anymore, I ask them to look at their life, and notice what else was happening when they stopped praying.

People who are honest and self-aware often notice that prayer lost its appeal when they started partying pretty heavily; or when making money started to take priority; or when they decided to move in with their boyfriend; or when they just got bogged down in problems and became so self-absorbed that they pushed God away.

Whatever the details, old-fashioned sin often creates an ever-widening gap in our relationship with God. The wider the gap, the less likely we are to pray. And the less we pray, the wider the gap becomes. But noticing the gap is the first step to closing it.

JOURNAL: *If you're no longer eager to pray, write about what else was going on in your life when you started drifting from God. Note any patterns of sin that might be standing between you and God. What can you do to change?*

Despising God's Name

"Where is the respect due me?" says the LORD Almighty.
"It is you, O priests, who show contempt for my name.
But you ask, 'How have we shown contempt for your name?'"
You weep and wail because [the LORD] no longer pays attention to your offerings. . . .
You ask, "Why?"

MALACHI 1:6; 2:13-14

God called his people on the carpet for not giving him the respect he deserved. Despite God's clear instructions to offer only the best animals as sacrifices to the Lord, the Israelites took the worthless animals—the blind, the lame, the ready to die—and brought them to God's altar.

Through Malachi, God exclaimed, "You blatantly sin against me and then have the gall to ask for favors? You rebel against me and then expect me not to be affected by your disobedience? Your sin breaks my heart. It feels like betrayal."

If we do not live in submission to God, we lose the sense of warmth and closeness with him. We may feel nostalgic about the prayer times we used to have, but we've put up a sin barrier that will have to come down before we can enjoy a loving relationship with him again. We can have no deep, ongoing fellowship with God unless we obey him—totally.

PRAY: *Ask God to show you the sin barriers you have constructed. Ask for his forgiveness for not obeying him.*

T H U R S D A Y *Broken Relationships*

Anyone who claims to be in the light but hates his brother
is still in the darkness.

1 JOHN 2:9

Unresolved relational conflict is a prayer buster. Most of us grossly under-estimate how committed God is to building and maintaining a loving commu-nity, a family. He adopts us into his family, and he wants us to carry our rela-tionship with him into our relationships with others. If we do good to our brothers and sisters, it is like doing good to Jesus himself (Matthew 25:31-46). Since God has forgiven us, we should forgive others (Ephesians 4:32; Colos-sians 3:13).

There's no point in trying to pray if we are engaged in ongoing conflict with a family member, a coworker, a neighbor, a friend. God will listen when you come out into the light, confess the sins that drove you and the other person apart and attempt to mend the relationship.

JOURNAL: *Do you treat your spouse or other family members with respect and consideration? Write a response to this question in your journal: how might the way that I treat my family members be hindering my prayers?*

When you ask, you do not receive, because you ask with wrong motives,
that you may spend what you get on your pleasures.

JAMES 4:3

Selfishness is a prayer buster. It inspires us to make many inappropriate requests. Selfishness in the heart is a very common barrier between the Christian and God.

How would you feel if your prayer requests were made public, displayed on a billboard? "Dear Lord, make me famous. Make me rich. Make sure I have a good time. Make all my dreams come true."

When I began to study prayer, I was devastated over this point. I found that I'd been saying, in effect, "Keep me from trial or tragedy or pain or anything that would make me really grow and become a man of God. Just give me a convenient, happy, satisfying, problem-free life." There was grand confusion between wants and needs, rights and favors, justice and grace, convenience and conformity to Christ.

When Jesus prayed the model prayer we call the Lord's Prayer, his first requests were that God's name be reverenced, that his kingdom come, that his will be done. That doesn't sound much like the self-centered, shortsighted prayers I'd been saying. That's why Jesus gave us a model—to protect us from prayer-busting selfishness.

APPLY: *What steps can you take to put God, rather than yourself, back in the center of your prayers?*

Hearing the Cry of the Poor

You cannot fast as you do today and expect your voice to be heard on high. . . .
Is not this the kind of fasting I have chosen: to loose the chains of injustice and
untie the cords of the yoke, to set the oppressed free and break every yoke?
Is it not to share your food with the hungry and to provide the poor wanderer with shelter—
when you see the naked, to clothe him, and not to turn away from your own flesh and blood?
. . . Then you will call, and the LORD will answer; you will cry for help,
and he will say: Here am I.

ISAIAH 58:4-9

The Israelites were wondering why God was not answering their prayers. They had even fasted—and he still did not listen. God told them their lack of compassion was hindering their prayers. God is committed to developing a people who will reflect his character in this world, and his character always expresses concern and compassion for the afflicted.

If your ear is open to the afflicted, God will keep his ear open to you.

APPLY: *Look for a small way to care for the poor this week. Visit a nursing home, help out in a soup kitchen, take an unemployed friend to lunch. Keep looking for ways to serve others.*

MONDAY

God Says, "Go!"

"Test me in this," says the LORD Almighty,
"and see if I will not throw open the floodgates of heaven
and pour out so much blessing that you will not have room enough for it."

MALACHI 3:10

If the truth were known, often you and I are the only obstacles standing in the way of our receiving a desperately needed miracle. Our requests may be right. The timing may not be a problem. But when our lives are wrong, God says, "Before I grant your request, I want you to grow. Put that sin away. Change your attitude. Stop that practice, end that pattern, get off that merry-go-round, reconcile that relationship, soften up your spirit, repent, receive forgiveness. Grow!" Probably none of us can understand how much God wants to change that impossible circumstance, touch that untouchable person, move that immovable mountain in our lives. We matter to him, and he wants to meet our needs and grant our requests if we will free him to do it. When our request is right, when the timing is right and when the person is right, God says, "Go!"

Nothing motivates people to develop their prayer lives more than answered prayers.

JOURNAL: *Where do you sense God is saying "Go!" to you today? How are you an obstacle to your own prayers?*

Trusting the Father

My heart is not proud, O LORD, my eyes are not haughty;
I do not concern myself with great matters or things too wonderful for me.
But I have stilled and quieted my soul; . . . like a weaned child is my soul within me.

PSALM 131:1-2

God is no more intimidated by childish demands for instant gratification than wise parents are. He simply shakes his head at our immaturity and says, "Kick and scream if you must, but you can't have what you want yet. Trust me. I know what I'm doing."

Be wary of insisting that you know better than God about when a prayer request should be granted. God's delays are not necessarily denials. He has reasons for his "not yets."

Sometimes God delays in order to test our faith. Do we think of him as a celestial vending machine that we should kick if we don't get an instant response? Or do we relate to him as a loving Father who will give us what we need when we need it? To build a courageous faith, we need to trust even when things don't seem to be going the way we want them to.

APPLY: *What would happen to your relationship with God if you did what the psalm above says: quiet your soul, stop demanding, let go of pride and realize God knows more than you do?*

Greater Miracles

My thoughts are not your thoughts, neither are your ways my ways. . . .
As the heavens are higher than the earth, so are my ways higher than your ways
and my thoughts than your thoughts.

ISAIAH 55:8-9

Sometimes God delays answering prayer so that we can develop character qualities such as endurance, trust, patience and submission—qualities that come only when we wait patiently and trust in his timing. A lot of spiritual gains come through pain, hurt, struggle, confusion and disappointment. If we had our way, though, how long would any of us put up with these character builders without asking God to remove them? We may not be able to see the reasons for the delay, but that isn't surprising. We are the creatures; God is the Creator. He knows what timing is best.

How often I have waited for months and even years for my prayers to be answered! Frequently I have wondered if God was saying "no," only to find out later that he was saying "not yet," so that he could orchestrate a greater miracle than I had the faith to pray for in the beginning. When the results are in, God's wisdom is clear.

JOURNAL: *Write about a time when God seemed to be saying "not yet" to your prayers. How did the situation ultimately turn out? What did you learn from the seemingly unanswered prayer?*

Inappropriate Requests

Jesus took Peter, James and John with him and led them up a high mountain,
where they were all alone. There he was transfigured before them.
His clothes became dazzling white. . . . And there appeared before them Elijah and Moses.

MARK 9:2-4

How does God answer prayer? If the request is wrong, God says, "No." Some prayer requests, no matter how well-intentioned, are inappropriate.

In the story above, Peter, James and John were awed to behold God's splendor just a few feet from where they were standing. Then Peter came up with a bright idea. Loosely translated, his request went like this: "Jesus, let us build shelters up here for you and Moses and Elijah. We'll be happy to stay on the mountain with you and bask in your glory."

Jesus' immediate response was effectively "no": a thick cloud enveloped them, cutting off further conversation. Jesus and the disciples still had work to do down in the plains where people lived. They couldn't stay on the mountaintop. Peter's request was inappropriate, and Jesus would not grant it. You know you are growing when you realize that some of your requests are inappropriate, and that "no" was the best answer God could give.

JOURNAL: *Look back through the prayers in your journal. How many of those that remain unanswered are inappropriate requests? Ask God to show you whether your requests are appropriate or not.*

Too Loving to Say Yes

In his heart a man plans his course, but the LORD determines his steps.

PROVERBS 16:9

Years ago, my church was looking to fill an important staff position. Our staff had been praying that God would show us the right person to fill the need. Then simultaneously we all thought of an individual who looked custom designed to fill the position.

The elders commissioned me to meet with the person and ask him to consider joining our staff. All during our lunch, I was praying, "Lord, should I ask him right now? Is this the time? You know how desperately we need a person to lead in this area."

As I was ready to launch into my presentation, it became apparent to me that God was saying, "No—don't ask him." I had no idea why, but by God's grace I decided not to issue the invitation.

Six months later we learned that there was deception in the life of that leader. His entire ministry crumbled around him, and even today he is disqualified from service. That could have happened in our congregation, and God could have been dishonored in our midst. When I heard the tragic story, I silently prayed, "Thank you, Jesus, for having enough love and concern for our body to just say no."

APPLY: *Think of a specific decision you are facing. Commit yourself to listening to God throughout the entire process.*

Wrong Requests

> *How can you say to your brother, "Let me take the speck out of your eye,"*
> *when all the time there is a plank in your own eye?*
> *You hypocrite, first take the plank out of your own eye,*
> *and then you will see clearly to remove the speck from your brother's eye.*

MATTHEW 7:4-5

The most famous wrong prayer request is this: "O God, please change the other person." Any time two or more Christian people have to relate closely to each other, somebody is likely to make this request.

Now it's often perfectly appropriate to pray that someone will change. After all, that's what we do when we pray for conversions, for hearts to be softened, for bad habits or addictions to be broken. But too often the motive behind such a request is not authentic concern for the other person.

A more genuine prayer might be this: "I don't want to face my own shortcomings. I don't want to work on this relationship. Instead, I want the other person to accommodate all my personal needs, so I'm asking you to change him or her." If you pray that kind of prayer, God may say no. Sometimes, that's the most loving answer he can give.

PRAY: *When you find yourself wanting to pray to change someone, pray this way:* God, what is the plank in my own eye? How do I need to change?

MONDAY *God's Glory or Mine?*

Do nothing out of selfish ambition or vain conceit,
but in humility consider others better than yourselves.
Each of you should look not only to your own interests,
but also to the interests of others.

PHILIPPIANS 2:3-4

There are plenty of inappropriate, self-serving prayers masquerading as reasonable requests. "Please give me this new account" may be a good request for account executives to make. There's nothing wrong in praying for help in business; we should bring all our concerns to God. But if our motivation is to show off in front of the other sellers, or to get rich in order to live lavishly, or to thumb our noses at supervisors who advised us not to go after the account, it's a wrong request and God is likely to say no.

Or pastors may pray, "O Lord, help our church grow." Surely God would want to honor that request! But if the pastors' real meaning is "I want to be a star with a big church, fancy programs and lots of media coverage," their requests are wrong. Self-serving prayers won't build your faith, but getting honest about your motives will.

APPLY: *Are you praying self-serving prayers? Think carefully about your motives when you pray.*

God's Protection

> *Turn from evil and do good; seek peace and pursue it.*
> *The eyes of the LORD are on the righteous and his ears are attentive to their cry.*

PSALM 34:14-15

We can fool ourselves into thinking selfish requests are appropriate, but we can't fool God. He knows when our motives are destructive, and he often protects us from them by saying no.

Before bringing a request to the Lord, it's a good idea to ask, *If God granted this request,*

- *would it bring glory to him?*
- *would it advance his kingdom?*
- *would it help people?*
- *would it help me to grow spiritually?*

By forcing us to look closely at our requests, prayer can purify us. When we conclude that our motives have been wrong, we can say, "Lord, forgive me. Help me grow. Help me present requests that are in line with your will."

If you have been praying diligently about a matter and have sensed resistance from heaven, I challenge you to review your request. It may be the problem. Whatever the reason, if the request is wrong, God says, "No!" But we need not worry: God may have something better in mind.

JOURNAL: *If you are still wrestling with why God said no to one of your prayers, use the questions above to examine your motives and your request.*

 *How Long?*

> *How long, O LORD? Will you forget me forever?*
> *How long will you hide your face from me?*
> *How long must I wrestle with my thoughts and every day have sorrow in my heart?*
> *How long will my enemy triumph over me?*

PSALM 13:1-2

Unspeakable tragedies afflict believers and nonbelievers alike. The righteous suffer and the innocent perish. Many Christians sense that God hears and empathizes with their prayers, but some requests remain unanswered. Why would an all-loving, all-powerful God deny valid requests from faithful believers?

We need to remember that despite the victory God has achieved over Satan in the ministry and resurrection of Christ, everything is not yet submitted to God. The enemy's years are counted and his end is sure. But in the meantime, he causes much suffering.

However, God will have the final say, and he will assert his universal sovereignty at Christ's second coming. Because of this ultimate victory, Christians have the assurance that those very prayers that remained unanswered in this life will receive spectacular vindication in eternity. Then, God "will wipe every tear from their eyes. There will be no more death or mourning or crying or pain, for the old order of things has passed away" (Revelation 21:4). What a faith-building promise!

PRAY: *Speak honestly to God about your sorrows and disappointments. Express your desire to trust him for the prayers that have not yet been answered.*

Not Yet

> *Be patient, then, brothers, until the Lord's coming.*
> *See how the farmer waits for the land to yield its valuable crop and how patient he is*
> *for the autumn and spring rains. You too, be patient and stand firm,*
> *because the Lord's coming is near.*

JAMES 5:7-8

If the timing is wrong, God says, "Slow." For most of us, this does not feel much better than no. We live in an instant society, always trying to do everything faster. Freeways and supermarkets have express lanes; film companies promise prints in one hour; and we think our computers need upgrading if they make us wait five seconds.

Parents know that children rank the words "not yet" as nearly the most awful in the English language, second only to the word "no." You're leaving on a five-hundred-mile trip in the car. Fifteen miles from home, voices from the back seat ask, "Are we there yet?" "Not yet," you say, and the groans and complaints begin.

How children hate that answer. And there's an impatient child in all of us, who wants God to grant every request, move every mountain right now. When the all-knowing, all-wise, loving heavenly Father deems it best to say, "Not yet," what is our response? Are we able to trust his wisdom?

APPLY: *What prayer of yours do you sense God is saying "not yet" to? Ask God to help you grow in patience.*

FRIDAY

Blessed is the man who perseveres under trial,
because when he has stood the test, he will receive the crown of life.

JAMES 1:12

We spend a lot of energy trying to avoid trials, but we actually ought to thank God for them. Adversity helps us develop endurance, and endurance is a powerful weapon to have in our character arsenal.

It pays to consider the high cost of quitting. So many people live with scars from having quit on something or someone. So many look back on their lives, shake their heads and ask, "Why did I cash in so easily?" It's almost always easier to quit than to endure, but many of us have paid dearly for giving up too soon.

We live in the instamatic era. Nowadays we demand overnight stardom, overnight success, overnight solutions, overnight marital bliss and even overnight spiritual maturity. If our expectations are not met overnight, we have a strong tendency to quit prematurely. Even if we are Christians, we give up on God's mission for our lives before we've really put it to the test. We are fast becoming a weak-willed people because we don't understand endurance. But endurance is essential for building a courageous faith.

JOURNAL: *List examples of times you quit something before finishing. Was there a high cost? How can you build your endurance to stick with a current situation you're tempted to give up on?*

God Works for Good

And we know that in all things God works for the good of those who love him,
who have been called according to his purpose.

ROMANS 8:28

As I drive onto our church campus each day, I am reminded of how much better God's plans are than my schemes.

Before we bought our land, we had been meeting in a movie theater. We had our sights set on buying a piece of land. We all gave everything we could, but our total fell $200,000 short. I was caught off-guard. I didn't just want to quit; I wanted to die. I couldn't imagine any more time in that dark, filthy movie theater.

Then we found out that the land we had tried to buy had just been decreed forest preserve. Had we purchased it, we would have had to surrender it, and our money would have been tied up for months. Then came the news that a doctor who owned another piece of land nearby was willing not only to sell it but to accept as a down payment the exact amount of money we had already raised. We had to sheepishly admit that God, in his wisdom, had brought something good out of our failed plans.

PRAY: *Ask God to show you how he's going to work for good in all things in your life. Pray that you'll be able to see things from his perspective.*

MONDAY *Don't Be a Sluggard*

How long will you lie there, you sluggard? . . .
A little sleep, a little slumber, a little folding of the hands to rest—
and poverty will come on you like a bandit and scarcity like an armed man.

PROVERBS 6:9-11

When I was a kid and my mom asked me to do chores, I was likely to say something like "At the next commercial, Mom," or "As soon as I finish putting this model together." If my father heard me, he'd say, "Do it now, Billy. Don't wait." That aggravated me at the time; I thought he was unnecessarily inflexible and unreasonable. Now I realize he was a wise man who was committed to steering his son off the path of the sluggard. How grateful I am that as an adult I never had to go through the pain of breaking the pattern of procrastination. My dad did me a huge service by demanding prompt and responsible action.

The book of Proverbs says that many of us are in danger of becoming sluggards, and it describes a progression that could, and probably would, put us on the sluggard's futile and fruitless path. The first step down that path is procrastination.

APPLY: *Do you have a tendency to procrastinate? What can you do to break that pattern? Today if you hear yourself saying, "I'll do it later," stop and make yourself do that task right away.*

No Excuses

The sluggard says, "There is a lion outside!" or, "I will be murdered in the streets!"

PROVERBS 22:13

The sluggard above comes up with an imaginative excuse for not going to work. Maybe he finds it more stimulating to conjure up a fascinating list of everything that could go wrong than to patiently work his way through the mundane list of tasks to be completed.

Then again, let's say there is a lion in the streets. So tell the guy to join the lion hunt! Only a sluggard would sit around for the rest of his life because there are dangerous obstacles in his way. There will always be lions in the street. There will always be frightening responsibilities, overwhelming challenges, heartbreaking disappointments. But only the sluggard will throw excuse after excuse in the face of life's demands.

Procrastination breeds procrastination. Excuses breed excuses. Laziness, sluggishness, indolence, slothfulness—whichever slow-moving word you choose—they all breed more and more of the same slimy stuff. It's a thick soup you're sinking into, and you'll end up stuck in a life of ruin. Yes, obstacles and challenges will always be there, but God will always be there, too, ready to help if we ask him.

APPLY: *How much energy do you waste coming up with excuses for lack of performance? What would happen if you channeled that energy into simply doing the things you need to do?*

> *Woe to you Pharisees, because you give God a tenth of your . . . garden herbs,*
> *but you neglect justice and the love of God.*
> *You should have practiced the latter without leaving the former undone.*

LUKE 11:42

Many of us who on the surface look like models of industry and diligence are suffering from a hidden disease called selective sluggardliness. Like the Pharisees who seemingly kept rules but neglected the most important things, we have little pockets of laziness that will ultimately bring pain and heartache, even ruin, into our lives.

I'm talking about a student who succeeds athletically and socially but fails to take academics seriously. Or the dad who sets sales records at work but fails miserably to respond to the emotional needs of his wife and children. Or church members who nod their heads when the pastor challenges them to a deeper commitment to God, but when Monday morning rolls around they're back to their casual Christian ways.

One reason selective sluggardliness is so deadly is that if other areas of our lives look good enough we can convince ourselves that we deserve to be let off the hook. But nine-out-of-ten diligence is self-deception. Don't let such things corrupt your faith.

PRAY: *Are you hiding an area of slothfulness behind your accomplishments in other areas? Ask God to show you the truth about yourself, and ask for his help in changing.*

One Area of Laziness

Eli's sons were wicked men; they had no regard for the LORD.

1 SAMUEL 2:12

Eli, a priest, was highly respected. People considered his life a clinic on how to live with integrity. But in his later years, his life and ministry unraveled because of one area of laziness: he wouldn't discipline his sons. Although he had good intentions of training them in the ways of godliness and integrity, it proved to be a more daunting challenge than he had anticipated. So he gave up. In time his little rascals became big rascals. The trouble they eventually caused led to the undoing of Eli's life.

My father died of a heart attack at age fifty-three. A bigger-than-life character, he was one of the most energetic and motivated men I have ever known. He started businesses, helped ministries, flew airplanes, drove motorcycles and sailed a forty-five-foot yawl across the Atlantic Ocean. He was disciplined and diligent in every area of his life, except one: caring for his body. He was lazy and careless about that his whole life. He paid no attention to diet or exercise. Nine out of ten isn't bad—unless the tenth one kills you. Following God and his wisdom can protect you from the tragedy of ignoring fatal problems.

APPLY: *Is there one area of your life where you are letting things slide? Could that one area of neglect be a fatal mistake?*

 *Relational Laziness*

Get rid of all bitterness, rage and anger, brawling and slander,
along with every form of malice. Be kind and compassionate to one another,
forgiving each other, just as in Christ God forgave you.

EPHESIANS 4:31-32

A number of years ago a friend of mine entered a difficult phase of his marriage. Rather than take the route of relational courage, he eventually divorced his wife. A few years later, he told me with regret, "I gave up the most important relationship in my life because of laziness. That's all it was. If I could, I'd set the clock back and do it all over again. And this time I wouldn't quit working."

It takes courage to take the initiative, to practice diligence in relationships. The stakes are high; the pain of loss is great. Yes, your efforts at reconciliation may be rebuffed, but more often than not they will be warmly welcomed and met with a sincere "I want to try too. Thanks for taking the initiative."

JOURNAL: *Write a covenant with God to show relational courage by continuing to work on your marriage, your friendships, your relationship with your children. Put your intentions to paper and reread them whenever you feel like giving up.*

Diligent hands will rule, but laziness ends in slave labor.

PROVERBS 12:24

Whatever you do, work at it with all your heart, as working for the Lord, not for men.

COLOSSIANS 3:23

The apostle Paul takes the wisdom of Proverbs a step further when he reminds us that our ultimate motivation for working diligently is to honor our true boss.

Are you "working with all your heart" at your place of employment, at home, at school? I am not asking if you're expending the necessary energy to do the tasks assigned you. Are you doing every project that comes your way to the best of your God-given potential, as if you were doing it for God himself, not just for your earthly boss? At your company, are you setting the standard for ethics, love, excellence and promptness? Are you demonstrating genuine concern for those you work with, even pointing them to Christ if you get the opportunity?

The wisdom of the Bible says that diligent workers will be rewarded by their peers, by their employers and by God. This is no shimmering promise of health and wealth and happiness; it's a simple but profound insight about the way life works. Diligent labor is the pathway to a meaningful, responsible and useful life.

APPLY: *Is the Holy Spirit prompting you to take some initiative—immediately—and begin working heartily as unto the Lord?*

MONDAY

High Stakes

> *Let us not give up meeting together, as some are in the habit of doing,*
> *but let us encourage one another.*
>
> HEBREWS 10:25

A little girl in our church has endured more than her share of life's hardships, and some of her few joys are the relationships she has with people at church. Her father, whom I have known for many years, decided that he'd rather sleep an extra hour on Sunday mornings than take his little girl to church.

If this man wants to be lazy, that is his choice; but I hated what his laziness was doing to his little girl. "Listen," I said to him, "I may have no right to tell you how to live your life, but what's happening in your little girl's life is breaking my heart. She needs to be reminded that God loves her, she needs the care of a loving Christian teacher, and she needs Christian friends."

He said, "Come on, Bill. Give me a break. I work hard. I need a day off." I wasn't buying it. "Get lazy in another area," I told him. "Don't get lazy in an area that affects the life and eternity of a precious little girl." Maybe he had only one area of laziness, but he was playing with high stakes.

PRAY: *Do you have a habit of laziness that is negatively affecting others? Ask God to help you change.*

Out of Tragedy

The cords of the grave coiled around me; the snares of death confronted me.
In my distress I called to the LORD; I cried to my God for help.
From his temple he heard my voice; my cry came before him, into his ears.

PSALM 18:5-6

What moves people out of their comfort zone to do something good, or to call on God? We often see spikes of volunteerism not after a stirring presidential speech or a gold medal at the Olympics or some other great victory. They typically come on the heels of horrendous defeat—tragic loss. That's God at his best—working with his back against a terrible calamity. Our relentlessly redemptive God works behind the scenes to raise something good out of the rubble heap.

In the United States during good times, more than half the population makes the decision not to worship at a church. But against the backdrop of a national calamity, church attendance goes up. No one rallies people into the churches; they come on their own. Why do they come? God reminds people during tragedies that we need his wisdom, his love, his strength. Victories don't produce this effect, but defeat does. It's then that we see how God works for good in all things.

JOURNAL: *Write about a time when difficulty drew you closer to God. Thank God for using that storm to work in your life.*

The Anchor of Our Souls

You, O LORD, keep my lamp burning; my God turns my darkness into light.
You give me your shield of victory, and your right hand sustains me;
you stoop down to make me great.

PSALM 18:28, 35

Tragedy teaches us afresh that life needs to be valued and celebrated. Tragedy reminds us that evil is alive and well, and that we need strength and wisdom beyond our own to overcome it. Tragedy reinforces the truth that courage and compassion are greater than complacency and isolationism, that unity is more important than pettiness. And tragedy recalls us to a deep and abiding faith in God as the only anchor that can steady us during rogue winds. Only God—only a relentlessly redemptive God—could do this quality of work.

So when trouble comes your way, open up your mind and heart, and say,

God, work in my life in these dark days.

Speak to me, God. I'm listening.

Teach me, God. I'm willing to learn.

Prompt me, God. I will obey.

Tell me what to do, and I'll do it.

With God's help, we can gain perspective in the midst of calamity and come out the other side better for having experienced it.

PRAY: *Pick one of the sentence prayers above that resonates with you. Spend some time quietly praying that sentence and listening for God's leadings.*

Why Storms?

My God, my God, why have you forsaken me?
Why are you so far from saving me, so far from the words of my groaning?

PSALM 22:1

In the mid-1980s, a British tall ship made an Atlantic crossing with twenty-eight people aboard, most of them high school students. A wind gust of phenomenal proportions struck the vessel from out of nowhere, and the ship sank, killing seventeen people. The accident was attributed formally to what is known as a rogue wind.

Have you ever had an unexpected blast of trouble? A rogue wind hits you without warning: a devastating medical report knocks you over; a pink slip shows up on your desk; divorce papers come to your door; the police call about your son; the bank calls in your note.

God can, and often does, bring good out of storms: people rally together and focus on what's really important in life, and some even come to faith. But despite the potential in storms for positive outcomes, most honest, thinking people still have occasional late-night ceiling-staring sessions: *Why storms at all? Why do they strike me or my family?* Or a bigger question: *Why didn't God—supposedly sovereign, all powerful, loving—step in and protect me? Why?*

JOURNAL: *Write about a time when you questioned your life's difficulties. Can you now see the purpose of your suffering, something you learned or a way that you grew?*

Strength in Trouble

For in the day of trouble he will keep me safe in his dwelling;
he will hide me in the shelter of his tabernacle and set me high upon a rock.

PSALM 27:5

When we live calamity-free for long periods of time, not only do we feel a kind of invincibility, but we slowly begin to take life itself for granted. We stop thanking God for the daily blessedness of it—for sunrises and sunsets, for spring rains and fall colors, even for our own lives. We grow complacent with our spouses, our kids, our parents, our friends. We get too accustomed to the privilege of living.

Then a day like Tuesday comes. Tuesday, September 11, 2001. I saw an interview with a father whose son was lost that day. The father told the reporter, "I would give everything I own if my son would walk through that door one more time."

In that simple statement, the father reminded me of the value of life. Several hours later, my son walked through the door to my study. I threw my arms around him: "I'm so glad you're home."

JOURNAL: *When a day of trouble comes your way, what is your response?*
Write about a time when a difficulty caused you to remember what it is that you
truly value.

> *When you pass through the waters, I will be with you;*
> *and when you pass through the rivers, they will not sweep over you.*
> *When you walk through the fire, you will not be burned; the flames will not set you ablaze.*

ISAIAH 43:2

When an act of random evil slams into my life, I grab the truth in Isaiah 43: we pass through waters, but they will not overwhelm us; we pass through flames, but they will not consume us. There are many other texts like this in Scripture, but here's the point (and I hang on to this with a white-knuckled grip): our good God limits the amount and the severity of evil that comes my way so that it stays within my capacity to endure it. And then, just as Isaiah promises, God stays with us. In my darkest moments I've felt God say, "You're okay. I'm here with a love that will not let you go."

PRAY: *Do you feel God's presence with you? Express your thanks. If you are struggling to experience God's presence in your life right now, then voice those feelings to God.*

MONDAY

Enduring Difficulties

The LORD is close to the brokenhearted and
saves those who are crushed in spirit.

PSALM 34:18

Sometimes we have to witness brokenness and pain to understand how precious life is. When we discover that friends from college days are divorcing and recall with pain their joyous wedding day, we are reminded to thank God for a faithful spouse. When we discover that a parent is dying, we are overcome with memories of all they have done in our lives and are finally able to express our feelings toward them. There is also pain we experience ourselves—getting laid off from a job, betrayed by a friend, diagnosed with a devastating illness. When we come face to face with devastation, we start to see life through stark new lenses.

And seldom can we turn the corner on a tragedy as quickly as we might like. How long does it take, for example, to finish grieving the loss of a loved one, to complete the search for a missing person, to rebuild a devastated life? No, once we've endured a tragedy, at some level we think and feel differently forever. We catch a glimpse of what a precious gift our life really is.

PRAY: *Are you in a time of difficulty? Pray the words of Psalm 34: Lord, be close to me; I am brokenhearted. Lord, save me; I am crushed in spirit.*

Tissue Paper, Not Brick

Let us fix our eyes on Jesus, the author and perfecter of our faith,
who for the joy set before him endured the cross, scorning its shame,
and sat down at the right hand of the throne of God.

HEBREWS 12:2

When I run laps at the gym and feel I've reached my quitting point, I'll often say, "I'm going one more lap. This quitting point is not made of brick; it's made of tissue paper, and I'm going through it."

Quitting points are not as solid as some people think they are. With God's help you can go through them more often than not, and every time you break through one, a victory is gained in heaven and in your life.

Quitting points are painful—Jesus knows that even better than we do. He endured all the way to the cross. Every time someone slapped his face or the whip tore his back open, all hell screamed, "Quit!" But by strength from above and by his own resolve, Jesus crashed through his quitting points and died the death that makes salvation possible for every human being.

God says to us every time we come to a quitting point, "Crash through it—I'll give you the strength. It's made of tissue, not brick."

APPLY: *What problem feels like a brick wall in your life? Ask God to help you crash through your quitting point and develop endurance.*

Moving On

> *Weeping may remain for a night, but rejoicing comes in the morning.*
>
> PSALM 30:5

Despite its brevity, life on earth is a scandalously gracious gift from the hand of a good God—a gift that should be sincerely celebrated each day by those of us whose hourglasses still contain some sand. Yes, we should enter into the sorrows of people who suffer, praying that God will console and comfort those who have endured a tragic loss, but then we need to move from there to once again celebrate life.

Those of us who have experienced suffering have to learn how to adapt to a new reality: life after tragedy. But that comes later. Generally in the moment of tragedy we are hit with an onslaught of pain and urgent questions. A wise friend told me once that our task during that onslaught is "to try to turn all of that data into something redemptive. If there's no learning that comes from the storms of life, then the tragedy is compounded." The work that requires the most mental rigor and spiritual discipline is to consider the whys that accompany the storms of life. It's a question we need courageous faith to ask, and to answer.

APPLY: *Think about a recent storm in your life. Did you learn anything from your time of difficulty? How can you turn that storm into "something redemptive"?*

God's Presence

A righteous man may have many troubles,
but the LORD delivers him from them all.

PSALM 34:19

This is a hard verse to deal with. We'd like to think a righteous person would have few troubles, not many. But think carefully about when we feel closest to God, so aware of his presence that if someone pointed a gun at us and said, "Deny God's existence or I'll shoot," we would say, "Pull the trigger. I can't lie. God is here with me."

I have felt closest to God in moments when the pain level was so high that I didn't think I could make it one more day. In those moments, I've felt God move in.

Psalm 23 reminds us that if we open ourselves to God's presence and power, we can make it through even the valley of the shadow of death. In fact, in those times of pain and struggle, we may feel closer to God than ever before.

JOURNAL: *Recall a time of pain in your life. Did you sense God's presence at the time? Looking back, can you see how God was near to you? Write a note of thanks to God for keeping the promise of his presence in difficult situations.*

Winning Through Losing

If anyone would come after me, he must deny himself and take up his cross and follow me.
For whoever wants to save his life will lose it,
but whoever loses his life for me and for the gospel will save it.

MARK 8:34-35

Tragedy involves loss and defeat, and there's a spiritual principle that, like loss and defeat, is particularly difficult for Western Christians to embrace. It's sometimes called the kingdom inversion principle; I sometimes call it winning through losing. It pertains to how God produces something good out of something bad. In the middle of horrendous catastrophe, God moves into action in curious, behind-the-scenes ways.

The 1980s were called the decade of greed. I watched a lot of my contemporaries doing a lot of winning—vocationally, educationally, financially. I wondered what effect all those external victories were having on these people's inner lives. Maybe they were losing their ability to relate lovingly and intimately to God, family and friends. Maybe they were losing a little character and a little courage along the way. They had forgotten, as people still do today, that to save your life, you've got to let go and follow God. It's the only way God can turn our trials into triumphs.

APPLY: *Where is God asking you to deny yourself? What do you think it means, specifically, to "lose your life" for Jesus? What might be the benefits?*

Blessed are the poor in spirit, for theirs is the kingdom of heaven.
Blessed are those who mourn, for they will be comforted.

MATTHEW 5:3-4

In 1987 I visited a church where the sermon that day was an unedited outpouring of the pastor's overflowing sorrows. His sixteen-year-old son's blood disease was getting worse, and his financial anxieties were keeping him awake at night. Even worse, his younger son had become so disillusioned by God's apparent absence that he had abandoned his faith. The pastor was embarrassed by his pain, but honest about it.

But I became suddenly aware of a palpable supernatural work of God. Tears of compassion and acceptance were pouring down people's faces. As soon as the service ended, this beaten-down pastor was held, hugged and prayed for, and people spontaneously wrote checks out to him. And before they left, they sang a hymn of faith with such sincerity that I suspected angels were helping.

I walked away thinking, *This guy is experiencing a horrendous loss, and there's this mysterious, wonderful spirituality happening that my heart was longing for. What's the deal?*

A few days later, I wrote these words in my journal: "I'm convinced that prosperity diseases more souls than adversity ever will."

A P P L Y : *How often do you find yourself praying for prosperity? While we don't need to pray for adversity, we can look for the gifts God hides within our times of difficulty.*

MONDAY

Discipline

The fear of the LORD is the beginning of knowledge,
but fools despise wisdom and discipline.

PROVERBS 1:7

Some people seem to succeed at everything they try. They have successful careers; they relate well to their families; they may be involved in church and community activities; they are active, growing Christians—they are even physically fit. When you get close to people like this and try to determine just how they manage to fulfill so much of their potential, you find that in almost every case one quality plays a significant role—discipline.

Discipline is one of the most important character qualities a person can possess. It plays a key role in developing every area of life. But how many highly disciplined people do you know? Can you quickly think of five people that are truly disciplined in all areas of their lives? Are you disciplined yourself? God has given me hundreds of acquaintances, and only a small fraction of them demonstrate discipline to a significant degree. Not that people do not want to be disciplined—they do. But discipline, I fear, is an endangered character quality. That's why it's something we ought to have the courage to develop.

PRAY: *Are you disciplined? Ask God to show you which areas of your life need greater discipline. Ask for his help in helping you grow in these areas.*

Delayed Gratification

Go to the ant, you sluggard; consider its ways and be wise!
It has no commander, no overseer or ruler,
yet it stores its provisions in summer and gathers its food at harvest.

PROVERBS 6:6-8

Scott Peck wrote in *The Road Less Traveled,* "Delaying gratification is a process of scheduling the pain and pleasure of life in such a way as to enhance the pleasure by meeting and experiencing the pain first and getting it over with." He adds, "It is the only decent way to live."

In the marketplace, people willingly put up with long hours, short vacations, repetitive tasks and minimal pay because they know that if they endure the entry-level discomfort for a while, the payoff will eventually come in the form of more flexible hours, higher pay, longer vacations, more responsibility and more interesting tasks. They are practicing delayed gratification.

In your spiritual walk, delayed gratification will build your faith. Practice it, and you'll see God at work. You'll be able to say, "If I discipline myself to spend ten or fifteen minutes early in the morning in a quiet place, getting a proper perspective on my walk with the Lord—writing down some thoughts, reading my Bible, listening to a tape, praying—the whole rest of my day seems much more satisfying."

APPLY: *How could you practice the principle of delayed gratification in your spiritual life?*

*"In your anger do not sin": Do not let the sun go down while you
are still angry, and do not give the devil a foothold.*

EPHESIANS 4:26-27

Discipline also pertains to the relational life, especially in marriage. Sometimes my wife, Lynne, and I get together with couples who are experiencing pain in their marriage. After talking with them, we often realize that, even if they have been married a long time, they are just now dealing with things that should have been taken care of during the first two or three years of marriage. As problems arose or conflicts surfaced between them, they would refuse to face them. Rather than endure present discomfort for the sake of future happiness, they pretended nothing was wrong.

The result of their lack of discipline, of course, was escalating discomfort that eventually became intolerable. They would have been much better off saying, "Let's go through the pain right now so that we'll have a longer time of pleasure ahead." This courageous approach is not easy, but the result is a strong and thriving marriage.

PRAY: *Is there any unresolved conflict in your marriage or another significant relationship? Ask God to give you the courage to lovingly address the issues, even if they are painful, to restore the relationship.*

Advance Decision Making

Let us not become weary in doing good,
for at the proper time we will reap a harvest if we do not give up.

GALATIANS 6:9

Physical health is very important to me. I come from a family with chronic heart problems, and trouble started showing up in my medical reports when I was fifteen. So, for me, there is no playing games with my health.

I understand intellectually that I must first endure the pain of running and weightlifting if I am going to experience the satisfaction of feeling well and being healthier. That is, I understand discipline. But understanding alone is not enough to improve my health; I must put my beliefs into practice. I practice discipline when I make the decision, in advance, to go to the health club.

If every day at 3:30 I made the decision whether or not to go work out, I would not work out very often. When it comes right down to the moment of packing up and leaving, I often don't feel like going. But I practice advance decision making. Because I have already decided to exercise, I go whether I feel like it or not. Afterward, I'm always glad I made that decision.

JOURNAL: *Write about habits that you have tried to implement and failed. Then write about a decision regarding your physical or spiritual health that you will make in advance, and stick with.*

Fulfilling Your Potential

Train yourself to be godly. For physical training is of some value, but godliness has value
for all things, holding promise for both the present life and the life to come.

1 TIMOTHY 4:7-8

Advance decision making is an important factor in our relationship with God. We know we are saved by grace and not by hard work or planning or discipline. But without practicing discipline, we will not grow spiritually any more than we would grow physically if we neglected the disciplines of eating, sleeping and exercising.

If you are interested in fulfilling your spiritual potential, it is essential that you begin to practice advance decision making. I have discovered three things that I must do if my spiritual life is going to flourish. First, I need to worship regularly at my church. Second, I need a daily time of personal interaction with the Lord. Third, I need fellowship with other believers in some type of Christian service. If I do not actively participate in these three endeavors, I wilt. I feel spiritually frustrated, and it seems as if God is not using me. Sooner or later every true believer comes to an understanding of what it takes for him or her to flourish as a Christian. And who of us wouldn't want to grow in this way?

A P P L Y : *Identify an area of your life you have trouble being disciplined in. How could advance decision making help you?*

Walking with God

> *No discipline seems pleasant at the time, but painful. Later on, however,*
> *it produces a harvest of righteousness and peace for those who have been trained by it.*

HEBREWS 12:11

There is not one disciplined person who would deny the truth of it: discipline in any form, inevitably, is painful. But the harvest, the payoff, the reward—that's also inevitable.

Had I not built my life on the principle of advance decision making, I probably would not be walking closely with God today. If I do not set aside a time for a daily private meeting with God, I tend to drift way off track spiritually. Instead of devoting myself to God's agenda, I become consumed with my own agenda. Instead of trying to figure out how to be a greater servant to my congregation, I start figuring out manipulative ways to get other people to do my bidding. So, many years ago I said, "God, I need to meet with you when I am most alert and clear-thinking. Because I am a morning person, I'm going to set aside the earliest moments of my day to meet with you. I'm not going to ask myself if I feel like doing that. I'm just going to do it." And God has honored that commitment.

JOURNAL: *Write a letter to God expressing your desire to meet with him regularly. What will you do to keep this commitment?*

M O N D A Y   *Serve Others*

> *Whoever wants to become great among you must be your servant,*
> *and whoever wants to be first must be slave of all.*
> *For even the Son of Man did not come to be served, but to serve,*
> *and to give his life as a ransom for many.*

MARK 10:43-45

I did not realize how much I had bought into today's misplaced values until, during college, I was shocked awake by a professor's statement: "True personal fulfillment never comes through self-gratification."

That is the most countercultural statement I have ever heard, I thought. *It flies in the face of everything I've been taught.* But, I began to realize, it does not fly in the face of Jesus' teachings. "If anyone would come after me," Jesus said, "he must deny himself and take up his cross and follow me. For whoever wants to save his life will lose it, but whoever loses his life for me . . . will save it" (Mark 8:34-35).

The world writes books with titles like *Think and Grow Rich.* If Jesus were writing for today's market, he might call his book *Love and Give Everything Away.* When you give yourself to God and serve his people in sacrificial love, you find a fulfillment and satisfaction the world never experiences.

JOURNAL: *Write about your own quest for personal fulfillment. Have you tried the self-gratification strategy? What would it mean to love as Jesus would?*

The Beauty of the Church

All the believers were together and had everything in common.
Selling their possessions and goods, they gave to anyone as he had need.

ACTS 2 : 4 4 - 4 5

Willow Creek has a food pantry open to people going through times of desperate need. During one food drive an older, well-dressed woman approached me after a service and said, "For several years my life was on an extremely positive track. I loved being able to fill my trunk with bags of groceries for the food drives." Then her chin began to tremble, and she continued, "But my circumstances have changed. . . . I can't bring even a single bag. . . . I had to go to the food pantry myself."

I put my arm around her shoulder while she cried. "The beauty of the church," I said, "is that those of us who are able are called to give to others graciously and generously, as you have done many times before. And those who are faced with a legitimate need are called to receive from others with a spirit of thankfulness, as you are doing now. Those who give do so with the humble realization that a change in circumstances could throw them into desperate need. That's what it means to live in fellowship in a community of faith."

APPLY: *Is God calling you to help others in your church community? Or to humbly receive help from others?*

Letting the Spirit Work

There are different kinds of gifts, but the same Spirit.
There are different kinds of service, but the same Lord.
There are different kinds of working, but the same God works all of them in all men.

1   C O R I N T H I A N S   1 2 : 4 - 6

Years ago, a group of volunteer car mechanics at Willow Creek set up an auto shop in the church maintenance building to fix the cars of single mothers who couldn't afford necessary auto repairs. The ministry expanded as some church members began donating their used cars to the church. Volunteers cleaned, repaired and detailed these donated cars and gave them to people who desperately needed reliable transportation. Hundreds of vehicles are donated each year to this ministry.

One family that donated a car left an assortment of papers on the dashboard: gift certificates for our church bookstore and food service center, coupons for car washes and oil changes, and a note that read, "You have no idea how much joy it is for our family to pass this blessing on to you." How well served was the person who received that car? How nourished was the collective soul of the family that gave it? How alive was the Spirit of Christ in the life of our church community?

APPLY: *It sometimes takes courageous faith to use your spiritual gifts for others. But you will breathe life into your church and your soul when you obey God's call to serve.*

THURSDAY *The Greatest Need*

But in your hearts set apart Christ as Lord.
Always be prepared to give an answer to everyone who asks you to give the reason
for the hope that you have. But do this with gentleness and respect.

1 PETER 3:15

While we are commanded by God to respond to the tangible needs of others with practical acts of care and compassion, there is an even greater good we can offer to others: an introduction to the God of the universe. What more pressing burden does any man or woman carry than the burden of separation from God through sin? What deeper need does a person have than to be reconciled to God through Christ? If we can help people understand the divine love manifested in the substitutionary death of Christ and the divine power manifested in the resurrection of Christ, we will have given them the ultimate gift.

JOURNAL: *Could you introduce someone to Jesus? Do you have the courage and words to give an answer for the hope you have in Christ? Write a short, concise introduction to Christ that you could easily share with someone.*

Don't Give Up

Let us not become weary in doing good,
for at the proper time we will reap a harvest if we do not give up.

GALATIANS 6:9

This verse has been my personal ministry motto for over two decades. One of the biggest hindrances to doing good is the discouragement that often sets in when we see little positive impact from our efforts or see the world getting darker and sadder despite our hard work. "What's the use?" we ask. "Why should I keep on doing my little part? Why should I bother to care? What good does it do?"

The temptation is to move from discouragement to cynicism to self-absorption. People who used to overflow with love and be active in good works begin withdrawing into the small world of self-protection and isolation. Given the heartaches and disappointments they have known, they believe withdrawal is justified; they think they are doing themselves a favor. But as their external worlds get smaller, their inner worlds shrivel too. In turning their backs on the needs around them, they have turned their backs on the needs of their own souls. But if we persevere in doing good, God promises rewards—a harvest—beyond what we could possibly imagine. Knowing that builds my faith.

P R A Y : *Do you feel like giving up? Do you see yourself becoming cynical? Ask God to empower you not to give up.*

Reward for Good Deeds

Then the King will say . . . "Come, you who are blessed by my Father;
take your inheritance, the kingdom prepared for you. . . .
For I was hungry and you gave me something to eat,
I was thirsty and you gave me something to drink, I was a stranger and you invited me in,
I needed clothes and you clothed me, I was sick and you looked after me,
I was in prison and you came to visit me. . . .
I tell you the truth, whatever you did for one of the least of these brothers of mine,
you did for me."

MATTHEW 25:34-40

In the economy of God, whenever we do good for anybody—a lonely widow in a nursing home, a repentant prisoner in a county jail, a hungry child in a Third World orphanage, a struggling single mother in a suburban neighborhood, a weary shopper in a supermarket checkout line, a lonely student lamenting his parents' divorce—it's as if we are doing it for Christ himself, and our act of goodness so penetrates his soul that it becomes permanently etched in the memory bank of heaven. It takes courage to reach out to others, but God promises to reward us when we do.

PRAY: *Pray about people you know who have needs. Ask God for the courage to step out of your comfort zone and offer them a tangible reminder of God's love.*

Fall

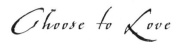

MONDAY

Choose to Love

And now these three remain: faith, hope and love. But the greatest of these is love.

1 CORINTHIANS 13:13

This oft-quoted verse tells us that despite the messages of our materialistic culture, the greatest legacy we humans can leave is the legacy of love. Whether we're speaking of our place within society at large or in the context of our primary relationships, the most valuable gifts we can offer are those thoughts and actions that flow from a loving heart.

To give these gifts requires us to choose to love, even when it is not easy. It is within the context of family that loving actions are most appreciated and necessary—and most difficult to maintain. We all have good intentions, but in the rough-and-tumble events of life we tend to bump and bruise each other. Even little wounds to our egos or our souls hurt, and often our natural reaction is to withdraw.

As emotional distance increases so does resentment. Soon a relationship of love has become a breeding ground for ill feelings. We know we should put an end to the discord. We should talk to the other person and try to resolve the problem. But we know how much time and energy it will take and how frustrating it may be. We know a true resolve will likely require an ongoing process rather than a single fix-it conversation. But a courageous faith is built by choosing to love, even when it gets complicated.

APPLY: *Who are some people that you are close to that you have perhaps bumped and bruised? Or who have hurt you in some way? How can you choose to love them?*

Stop the Hostility

The LORD looked with favor on Abel and his offering,
but on Cain and his offering he did not look with favor.
So Cain was very angry. . . . Cain attacked his brother Abel and killed him.

GENESIS 4:4-5, 8

A friend of mine is a paramedic in a Chicago neighborhood notorious for its gangs. "You know how it goes," he told me. "It starts with a little misunderstanding. It escalates when someone gets his feelings hurt and uses a little sarcastic language. His sarcasm provokes a smart-aleck response, which elicits a threat and then a challenge. Now the male bravado and honor get going. And then come the fists and the clubs and the knives and the guns. The blood flows and the flesh tears, and when it's all over and people are lying in piles, they call us and we come in and pick up the pieces."

I know how it goes. The cycle of hostility started with Cain and Abel, and it will take radical, nonretaliatory, second-mile lovers to stop it. Somebody has to take a blow, insult or slap instead of returning it. God says, "You can do it, if you're willing to become a radical lover." Are you willing?

A P P L Y : *You may not kill anyone, but what type of retaliation do you use? Perhaps backstabbing gossip, exclusion, unkind words? What would it take to be a "radical lover"?*

You have heard that it was said, "Eye for eye, and tooth for tooth."
But I tell you, do not resist an evil person.
If someone strikes you on the right cheek, turn to him the other also.
You have heard that it was said, "Love your neighbor and hate your enemy."
But I tell you: Love your enemies and pray for those who persecute you.

MATTHEW 5:38-39, 43-44

Evil is going to happen, and when it does, we can choose to perpetuate the cycle of retribution or to pursue reconciliation.

The Bible tells us that Jesus was illegally and falsely accused, illegally arrested, beaten and nailed to a cross. At any time during this process he could have called on ten thousand legions of angels to come and destroy those who were violating his rights and torturing his body. But he didn't. Instead he said, "Father, forgive them. They don't know what they're doing" (see Luke 23:34). Then he voluntarily went to the cross and procured the means of redemption for his executioners.

Rarely does the world follow Jesus' wisdom in situations like these, and the world is the worse for it. That's why God calls his followers to go against the tide, and to pursue reconciliation.

APPLY: *Call or write a letter to someone who has hurt or wronged you, expressing forgiveness and your desire for reconciliation.*

 *Handling Your Enemies*

Turn from evil and do good; seek peace and pursue it.

PSALM 34:14

Sometimes by the nature of my position, I find myself in the center of controversy: people misjudge or misrepresent my words or the activities of our church. You may find yourself in similar situations in your workplace or family.

I carry around with me one quote from Abraham Lincoln that helps me in such situations: "I have learned that the single best way to handle my enemies is to . . ."

Care to guess? It's not to kill them. Not to intimidate them. Not to seek revenge on them. Lincoln's approach to his enemies was "to figure out a way to turn them into friends." Once your enemies become your friends, you have no enemies to deal with. Problem solved. This quiet wisdom, which Lincoln attributed to Jesus, began the healing process as the American Civil War ended.

As leaders and everyday people around the world consider the teachings of Jesus, maybe—just maybe—we will respond to evil with acts of peace instead of ever-escalating acts of retribution and revenge. The Bible promises that if we are peacemakers, we'll be blessed.

JOURNAL: *List five steps you could take to turn an enemy into a friend. Explain why following these steps would be difficult but rewarding. Select one item from your list to try this week.*

Live at Peace

If it is possible, as far as it depends on you, live at peace with everyone.

ROMANS 12:18

Of course it isn't always possible to have authentic relationships. Sometimes the other person would rather continue the warfare than accept your apology. If this happens, look deep into your heart. Have you sincerely tried to restore the relationship, or are you holding something back? Do you really want restoration, or would you rather blame the other person and let the rupture continue? If your attempts have been wholehearted and honest, God will not let the broken relationship stand in the way of your prayers. But if your reconciliation attempts have been halfhearted and self-serving, try again—this time for real. It not only takes courage to restore relationships, but courageous faith as well.

PRAY: *If there is a relationship that needs help in your life, ask God for courageous faith, and for supernatural healing to occur in that relationship.*

Clinging to Christ

If the LORD delights in a man's way, he makes his steps firm;
though he stumble, he will not fall, for the LORD upholds him with his hand.

PSALM 37:23-24

When you take slaps, give up your legal rights and carry baggage a lot farther than you need to, you find yourself out in deep water with Christ. Realizing that the ground is not solid beneath your feet, you cling to him. You feel his support in ways you would normally never notice. Most people never leave the harbors of love. They are afraid to venture out on the high seas of radical, nonretaliatory, second-mile love. But that's where the action is.

When you let God make your steps firm, that's courageous faith. That's where God's presence manifests itself in a far greater way than shorebound people could ever imagine. That is where people are startled into taking a closer look at Jesus Christ, the world's only perfect example of radical love. That is also where hostilities die and lasting peace begins.

Radical love does not make sense. It is not easy. But it is something that the world desperately needs. And Jesus is calling his followers to love in that way.

PRAY: *Ask God if there is a situation where you need to take a risk, love radically and experience God's presence in a new way. Ask for the courage to take that risk.*

MONDAY *Courageous Faith*

God did not give us a spirit of timidity, but a spirit of power.

2 TIMOTHY 1:7

I've always been fascinated by courage. When I was a boy, my dad bought a sailboat in Ireland and sailed it back across the Atlantic Ocean through a hurricane. Before leaving home, he read books so that he would know what he was in for. Many of these were books about disasters at sea, and they all included a scene where people were lined up on the deck as the ship went down, wondering what to do because there were not enough life jackets to go around. Some guy would always say, "Here, take mine." As I read that, my breath would get short and my pulse would start to race.

Whenever I hear of someone showing courage instead of cowardice, I find myself saying, "That's what I want to be like." I wish I had more courage. I do not want to be debilitated by fear or paralyzed by anxiety. I do not want to cave in under difficult circumstances and compromise my convictions or give up on difficult challenges. I do not want to be a coward; I want to be courageous.

JOURNAL: *Write about some difficult circumstances or challenges you are facing. How could you handle these situations courageously? What barriers get in your way of being courageous?*

Facing Your Fear

God is our refuge and strength, an ever-present help in trouble.
Therefore we will not fear, though the earth give way and the
mountains fall into the heart of the sea.

PSALM 46:1-2

You grow in courage when you face your crippling fears. Sometimes we think courageous people were born without fear. In actuality, courageous people are ordinary people like you and me who began at some point to face their fears rather than running from them.

When I was growing up, my dad saw that I was a timid guy, and so he always challenged me to do things I was afraid to do. When I was in grade school, for example, he'd take me down to our produce company and bark out, "Billy, go out and back in that semi." I'd been driving tractors for several years, but I'd drag myself into the cab of that forty-foot rig, just shaking with fear. Sometimes it would take me forty-five minutes, and the truck would be half-jackknifed against the dock. But when I crawled out, my knees shaking, Dad would say, "Good job." The next time he would ask me to do it, it would be just a little bit easier.

PRAY: *What do you fear most? Ask God to help you take small steps to overcome your fear. Don't be afraid to do what your loving Father asks of you.*

Good Company

> *Bad company ruins good morals.*
>
> 1 CORINTHIANS 15:33 NRSV

If you really want to become more courageous, you'll need to surround yourself with good models. If you spend time with spineless people, you will probably become spineless yourself. Unfortunately, we are often surrounded by people who cave in, quit, compromise and play it safe as part of their daily routine. But if you want to grow in courage, make a calculated choice to increase your exposure to courageous people. Read autobiographies of courageous people; articles about courage; and Bible stories about people like Moses, Daniel, Esther and Paul who, though petrified, went ahead in faith and grew. When I read these stories, I'm inspired to grow in courage.

JOURNAL: *Look in the Bible for the stories of the people mentioned above. Write down the specific things each one did to act courageously. Write down one or two things you could do to emulate these people. Make a list of other courageous people you could talk to or read about.*

THURSDAY

Courage in the Ordinary

Have I not commanded you? Be strong and courageous.
Do not be terrified; do not be discouraged,
for the LORD your God will be with you wherever you go.

JOSHUA 1:9

Every single day we make choices that show whether we are courageous or cowardly. We choose between the right thing and the convenient thing, sticking to a conviction or caving in for the sake of comfort, greed or approval. We choose either to take a carefully thought-out risk or to crawl into a shrinking shell of safety, security and inactivity. We choose either to believe in God and trust him, even though we do not always understand his ways, or to second-guess him and cower in corners of doubt and fear.

These choices come our way every day, rapid fire. We face them so frequently that we forget that we are even making them, and we sometimes find ourselves going with the flow instead of carefully making courageous choices. The older I get, the more I understand that it takes a great deal of courage to face life's ordinary, everyday challenges.

APPLY: *Where in your life are you having trouble doing the right thing, making the courageous choice? Are you allowing God to be involved in that part of your life? If not, why not? Pray that he would help you to make courageous choices.*

Truth~Telling Courage

Therefore each of you must put off falsehood and speak truthfully to his neighbor.

E P H E S I A N S   4 : 2 5

At the beginning of every semester, professors say, "On such-and-such a date, your term paper will be due." But it is easy to get sidetracked, and when the due date is tomorrow, you suddenly realize that your paper is not ready. You go to the teacher's office and say, "Prof, you wouldn't believe what happened to me. My Aunt Ethel took ill, the library lost the one reference book I most needed, and the dog ate the final draft of my paper right after I pulled it out of the typewriter." You say anything but the truth, hoping the professor will be merciful.

Very few students walk into the professor's office and say, "You made an assignment several months ago. It was fair, and I understood it clearly. Unfortunately, I played too many hands of cards and too much racquetball. I was undisciplined, and I procrastinated. Now I don't have the assignment done. I make no excuses; it was my fault. Do whatever you think is right." Why don't people operate that way? Because it is painful to own up to the truth about our behavior. It takes courage.

J O U R N A L : *Write about a time when you had to own up to the truth about your behavior. Did you tell the truth? What can you learn from your past mistakes?*

Courage to Follow

We live by faith, not by sight.

2 CORINTHIANS 5:7

In all your ways acknowledge him, and he will make your paths straight.

PROVERBS 3:6

We used to play a game at summer camp in which we would blindfold one of the kids and have him or her rely on a friend for verbal directions to help navigate. "Turn to the left; there's a tree coming!" "There's a log in front of you—jump!" Some kids would not trust the verbal directions whatsoever. They would shuffle their feet and walk very slowly, even though their friends were shouting that the way was clear. Other kids would trot along, and a few would go like gangbusters. All the kids, though, had to fight the urge to tear off the blindfold so that they could see what was ahead. It takes a great deal of courage to follow another person's lead.

As Christians, we sometimes feel like those blindfolded children. Following Jesus Christ demands an enormous amount of courage. Quite often his leadings sound illogical, irrational, countercultural. Sometimes he is so challenging that I say, "No, I think I'll just play it safe." Then a voice inside me says, "Where's your courage, Hybels? Get up and walk. You can trust God."

PRAY: *Identify an area where you have trouble trusting God. Pray for the courage to follow God's leadings and walk with confidence in him.*

M O N D A Y   *Courageous Marriage*

*For this reason a man will leave his father and mother and be united to his wife,
and they will become one flesh.*

GENESIS 2:24

I try not to give two-cent answers to hundred-dollar questions, but when people ask me what it takes to build a meaningful marriage, I say, "Courage."

It takes an enormous amount of courage to say to your spouse, "Our marriage is in serious trouble, and we've got to do something about it."

What do most people do? They put their problems on the back burner. While they pursue their own careers and their own recreations, the marriage disintegrates from lack of courage. They did not have the courage to put on the gloves and say, "Let's fight for this marriage. Let's go to a marriage retreat. Let's see a marriage counselor. Let's lay it out on the table and solve these problems instead of running from them." It takes courage to fight off the "greener grass" temptations, to work through layer after layer of masks, cover-ups and defense mechanisms, to keep working on that marriage year after year. It is these steps of courage that create the intimacy that allows a marriage relationship to flourish.

APPLY: *Talk with your spouse, or significant other. Each give an honest assessment of your relationship; then have the courage to work through whatever issues or conflicts you are facing.*

Relational Courage

A wise son heeds his father's instruction,
but a mocker does not listen to rebuke.

PROVERBS 13:1

It takes relational courage to raise kids. How often I see parents backing off from proper discipline because they don't want to endure their kids' disapproval! The kids throw a tantrum and say, "I hate you," and the parents give in. If you want to raise your children the way God wants them raised, you will have to let the little tyrants get mad. Show some courage and say, "You don't intimidate me, little one. This is the right thing to do, and this is what you're going to do."

It also takes relational courage to build significant relationships with friends, to look another person in the eye and say, "Isn't it time we stopped talking about the weather and the stock market and started talking about what's going on in your life and mine?" Not many of us have the courage to challenge each other, to fight for each other's spiritual and relational growth. But these are the tasks that bring us into true Christian friendship. And it's well worth the risk.

JOURNAL: *Write the names of three people (friends, family, etc.) that you'd like to have a better relationship with. Brainstorm some ideas in your journal of ways you could show relational courage to move toward deeper intimacy or respect with each person on your list.*

Avoid Sexual Temptation

For the lips of an adulteress drip honey . . .
but in the end she is bitter as gall. . . . Now then, my sons, listen to me. . . .
Keep to a path far from her, do not go near the door of her house.

PROVERBS 5:3-4, 7-8

If you want to avoid sexual sin, you need to decide ahead of time to avoid sexual temptations. In this passage, a father warns his sons, "Don't get near the loose woman's house. Don't walk down her street. Decide now that you won't go there."

I can imagine this father taking his discussion a step further. "Make your decision now, in broad daylight, while your thinking is clear and your mind is in control of your body. Consider the consequences of your actions. Look both at the benefits of sexual purity and at the high costs of sexual sin. Consider the value of having a clean conscience before God. Consider the value of maintaining your integrity before your friends. Consider the value of not having to worry about sexually transmitted diseases and unwanted pregnancies."

I think this father knew that if his sons failed to decide ahead of time to avoid sexual temptation, they would probably yield to it eventually, and live with regrets.

APPLY: *What decisions about your sexual purity can you make today that will help you avoid painful circumstances in the future?*

> *Do not conform any longer to the pattern of this world,*
> *but be transformed by the renewing of your mind.*
> *Then you will be able to test and approve what God's will is—*
> *his good, pleasing and perfect will.*

ROMANS 12:2

You grow in courage as you allow your mind to be transformed. Sooner or later you begin to understand the centrality of courage in all walks of life. Courage is not an isolated, optional character quality. It is not merely a nice trait for people who want it but unnecessary for those who are not interested in it. Courage is foundational to being a Christian.

It takes courage to begin a walk with Christ, to reach out your hand and trust him. It takes courage to lead a life of obedience to Christ. It takes courage to be moral and to build significant relationships with your spouse, your children and with your friends. It takes courage to expand a business, change your major or start a new career. It takes courage to leave home or to go back home.

Courage—we all need it, and God wants us to have it.

PRAY: *Where do you find yourself tempted to "conform to the pattern of this world"? Confess your struggles to God, and ask him to help you courageously live a life of obedience.*

A Tainted Cosmos

For the creation was subjected to frustration . . .
in hope that the creation itself will be liberated from its bondage to decay
and brought into the glorious freedom of the children of God.

ROMANS 8:20-21

The Scriptures clearly indicate that natural calamities were not God's intention for the world. One of the consequences of Adam and Eve's sin was the infiltration of evil into the natural order. The entire cosmos is tainted by the effects of evil.

Most theologians hold the view that God created the natural universe to operate according to physical laws—gravity, motion, friction, inertia and so on. God allows a great measure of freedom within these basic laws. When somebody asks, "Why did God make it rain on my wedding day?" the answer is probably, "A low-pressure system combined with moisture from the Gulf of Mexico."

There's a lot of room in the natural order for events to simply unfold. God set up natural laws, and in order for those natural laws to have any real meaning—for nature to have any function—the clouds may do things that frustrate our plans from time to time. But the God who created clouds is still good.

APPLY: *Do you find yourself blaming God for natural calamities? What evidence do you see of the cosmos being tainted by evil? What evidence do you see in your own heart?*

Decision Makers

Be very careful, then, how you live—not as unwise but as wise,
making the most of every opportunity, because the days are evil.

EPHESIANS 5:15-16

I remember a theology class in my college years when a frustrated student shouted from the back of the room, "Why doesn't God put an end to all the evil deeds being done in this depraved world?"

The professor smiled and said, "He certainly could. He has the power. But the moment he keeps your fist from punching me in the nose, the human experiment—the human experience—is over. If God steps in and averts evil deeds whenever they pop up, we all revert to divine automatons. We have no self anymore. We lose our ability to think and act. Even love loses its meaning, as do qualities like courage, honesty, loyalty and steadfastness, because there's no choice anymore."

We can't have it both ways. We can be puppets and live in a world without pain, or we can be decision makers and live in a world where our bad decisions harm us and the people around us and break the heart of God. It's one or the other. But with God's help, we can reject evil and choose good.

APPLY: *Rather than decrying the evil in the world, examine your own heart. Have you been careful with how you live? Are you loving? courageous? honest?*

M O N D A Y *God the Risk Taker*

I have set before you life and death, blessings and curses.
Now choose life, so that you and your children may live and that you may
love the LORD your God, listen to his voice, and hold fast to him.

DEUTERONOMY 30:19-20

In the beginning, God took a risk of unimaginable proportions by giving human beings free will, the capacity for autonomous decision making. God knew that doing so was fraught with risk. It's like giving a fifteen-year-old kid the keys to a Ferrari. Lots of bad stuff could very well happen. God promised blessings to his people if they followed his ways, but they didn't always do so.

But putting puppet strings on the arms and legs and wills of his magnificent creations, reducing them to marionettes who would respond to his tugs dutifully but without passion, without feeling, meant creating conscious beings without a sense of self. God chose the risk of free will, and human beings since then have established a checkered track record, at best, with regard to decision making.

All of us have fumbled the free-will ball. The amazing thing is that God is willing to love us into people who can not only handle free will, but will choose freely to love him back.

PRAY: *Talk to God about times that you've fumbled the free-will ball, and pray for strength to use this amazing gift with integrity.*

Don't Abuse Grace

What shall we say, then? Shall we go on sinning so that grace may increase?
By no means! . . . For we know that our old self was crucified with him
so that the body of sin might be done away with, that we should no longer be slaves to sin.

ROMANS 6:1-2, 6

When rogue winds strike me, I tend to cry out, "Why, God? Why are you allowing this? Why aren't you protecting me better?" But when I think through the trouble, sometimes I learn that I am the cause of a certain amount of my pain. Not God—me.

One morning, I visited the jail cell of a friend who had been in prison for ninety days. Because I'm a pastor, he said, "Oh Bill, why me? Why would God allow this to come into my life?" I let him talk for a while, and then I asked him some questions.

"Just out of curiosity, did you know that what you did was against the law?"

"Well, yes."

"Was this your first offense?"

"No."

Hmmm. It's not easy to admit that we cause some of the pain in our own lives, but doing so is the first step toward healing.

JOURNAL: *Write about a current situation where you're asking, "How could God do this?" List five things YOU have done that may have caused at least some of the problem.*

Evil and the Evil One

*Be self-controlled and alert. Your enemy the devil prowls around
like a roaring lion looking for someone to devour.*

1 PETER 5:8

We can't have an honest conversation about suffering and tragedy without the acknowledgment of the role of the evil one. A lot of people disagree with my take on how the world works, and I've taken my share of ridicule for believing in the presence and the power of an evil being. But the Bible teaches unequivocally that the evil one carefully devises a variety of sinister plans for the express purpose of destroying people's bodies, minds and souls.

If the mission of Jesus is to forgive the sins of wayward people, the mission of the evil one is this: he's seeking someone to mess with. Jesus talked about this: "The evil one comes to kill, steal, and destroy. I have come to give life in all its fullness" (see John 10:10). When we acknowledge the existence of evil, we see more clearly our need for the perfect goodness and life that only Jesus offers.

APPLY: *Spend some time looking up passages in the Bible that talk about Satan. Then take a look at the world and its pain and suffering. What conclusion can you draw? Is there an evil being at work in the world?*

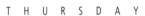

Evil at Work

As for you, you were dead in your transgressions and sins,
in which you used to live when you followed the ways of this world and of the ruler of the
kingdom of the air, the spirit who is now at work in those who are disobedient.

EPHESIANS 2:1-2

Not long ago, I was talking to a woman whose demeanor was so troubled that I couldn't resist saying, "Tell me about what's gone wrong in your life." Out the story came.

When she didn't give her husband the food he wanted, the service he expected or the sex he demanded, he would spin his handgun on the kitchen table, in plain view of their kids. The message was clear: "You'd better give me what I want." What motivates a middle-aged, well-educated, professional man to do something like that?

Who prompts an adult to sell drugs to kids? Who prompts a person to open a kiddy porn site on the Internet? Who prompts terrorists to slaughter innocent people and call it a holy campaign?

Some rogue winds are simply carefully planned attacks by the evil one, designed to wreck our faith, our marriages, our families, our churches, our communities. We have to intellectually respect this to defend ourselves, and we can do it—with God's help.

PRAY: *Ask God to help you understand the true nature of evil, and to help you stand firm against it.*

F R I D A Y   *Overcoming Evil*

Do not be overcome by evil, but overcome evil with good.

ROMANS 12:21

Obviously, evil is alive and well—in the world and in us. That being the case, our task is to figure out how to restrain the power of evil—how to loosen its grip on us. For generations the forces of evil have deceived us into thinking that ever-increasing levels of retaliation will eventually straighten out the disagreements that arise between people groups. But has that strategy been effective in the Middle East? in Northern Ireland? in the Sudan? Rather than quelling hostility, that strategy seems to escalate it to the point that blood is flowing like a river.

Sometimes evil gets so entrenched that drastic action is the only adequate response. But if we keep returning evil for evil, eventually our planet will be filled with people eating, drinking and sleeping hatred and violence. We must ask God for help in loosening evil's grip on our hearts.

PRAY: *Think of someone who has wronged you. How could you return good for evil? Pray for God to help you love that person, not just in your thoughts but also in your actions.*

Inhuman Humanity

In his arrogance the wicked man hunts down the weak,
who are caught in the schemes he devises.
He boasts of the cravings of his heart; he blesses the greedy and reviles the LORD.
In his pride the wicked does not seek him; in all his thoughts there is no room for God.

PSALM 10:2-4

Sometimes our trouble is caused by some other human being's depravity. The first time this came into focus for me was at a Christian summer camp when I was about eight. My father shipped me off to this camp, giving me five dollars as spending money for two weeks. Three days into the camp session, someone broke into my suitcase and stole my money. I called home and told my dad the whole story. After listening, he said, "Billy, there are bad people in this world. This won't be the last time someone rips you off. That's the kind of world you're living in. Get used to it." He was such a tender man.

I began to understand the implications of living on a planet with other depraved human beings whom God has given a free will. People do evil things. Depravity is on the loose.

JOURNAL: *Write about a time you encountered the depravity of another human being in a way that affected you personally. Do you agree that "depravity is on the loose"? Why or why not?*

M O N D A Y   *Transforming Love*

> *The people walking in darkness have seen a great light;*
> *on those living in the land of the shadow of death a light has dawned.*

ISAIAH 9:2

We all are now vulnerable to the depravity of every single human being. Someone in one corner of the world can bark out an order that results in a wave of death on the other side of the planet. That makes the work of the church more urgent than ever. Our world desperately needs churches to reach into their communities with the transforming love of Jesus Christ, so that more and more people will begin living their lives in conformity with the teaching and example of Jesus.

What if a few billion more people, in the next few years, were to come into a saving relationship with Jesus Christ? What if they were to choose love over hate, peace before violence? This planet could become a decent place to hang out.

Jesus told us to pray that God's will would operate on earth the way it does in heaven (Matthew 6:10). But earth will become a reflection of heaven only as we lead people into a transforming relationship with God. It's the only solution for the world, and for each of us.

PRAY: *Pray Matthew 6:10, "Your will be done, on earth as it is in heaven." Ask God how you can help bring his light into this dark world.*

Serve One Another in Love

Do not use your freedom to indulge the sinful nature; rather, serve one another in love.
The entire law is summed up in a single command: "Love your neighbor as yourself."
If you keep on biting and devouring each other, watch out or you will be destroyed by each other.

GALATIANS 5:13-15

Imagine a graph with a blue zone on the left, representing truth, a yellow zone on the right, representing love, and a green zone in the middle, where truth and love mingle. Where would you place yourself on that continuum?

Do you live in the yellow zone? Are you proud of your reputation for always offering a word of encouragement and freely spreading love and grace around? But do you shrink back from speaking words of truth? Do you pursue peace-keeping at the expense of truth telling?

Or are you a sharp-edged person who prides yourself on living in the blue zone? Are you fearless when it comes to slapping people with necessary truth? Do you enjoy "fixing people"? But do you generally ignore that bit about kindness, love and grace?

The challenge is to move toward the green zone and develop the supernatural ability to communicate truth with such a kind spirit that your words become a channel for God's transforming power.

JOURNAL: *Draw yourself on this continuum. Write down three steps you could take to move toward the green zone.*

What's Your Motive?

When you give a luncheon or dinner, do not invite your friends,
your brothers or relatives, or your rich neighbors; if you do,
they may invite you back and so you will be repaid.
But when you give a banquet, invite the poor, the crippled, the lame, the blind,
and you will be blessed. Although they cannot repay you,
you will be repaid at the resurrection of the righteous.

LUKE 14:12-14

Jesus knows how easily we deceive ourselves about why we do what we do. He knows how quick we are to pat ourselves on the back for a selfless good deed when in reality we're engaged in a favor exchange program that has little, if anything, to do with true goodness.

It happens all the time in my community. People with huge homes invite other affluent people to extravagant dinners, hoping that the favor will be returned. Usually it is, and the mutually beneficial pattern continues. There's nothing wrong with throwing such dinner parties, but they have little to do with true goodness. Rather than giving so that others can give back to us, why not try giving to those who can't return the favor, so that God can be the one who pays us back?

APPLY: *This week, do something for someone who cannot return the favor. What does it feel like to act in an unselfish way?*

Welcome the Needy

He who oppresses the poor shows contempt for their Maker,
but whoever is kind to the needy honors God.

PROVERBS 14:31

Just down the road from my church is a residential center for mentally hand-icapped adults. According to Jesus, a true-goodness dinner party might in-volve picking up four or five such residents and serving them a lovely dinner in one's own home. Or it might mean taking senior adults from a nursing home to a community event and then out for dessert at a local restaurant. Another idea is to throw a party or plan an outing for a group of physically or mentally challenged children. Imagine a dinner party that nourishes your own heart, as well as the bodies and hearts of children who all too often find themselves in our culture's most neglected category. Many churches and communities have programs through which caring adults and families can provide hospitality, friendship or a simple conversation to those who could never return the favor.

What would happen if you were to invite a few people outside the normal circle of your friends, a few people who don't usually get invited, a few people like the ones Jesus might invite, to your next social function? Honoring God sometimes requires more than pious words. It requires bold action.

JOURNAL: *Write about whether you find yourself resonating with these ideas, or resisting them.*

A kind man benefits himself, but a cruel man brings trouble on himself.

PROVERBS 11:17

Our souls are nourished when we are kind. That's not the only motivation for doing good, but it's an undeniable benefit.

I remember one winter when my kids were young and we had a huge snowstorm. We were out shoveling our driveway when I noticed that the driveway of our neighbors, who were going through a difficult time, had not been shoveled. So, after we had cleared our driveway, I dragged the kids and their miniature shovels next door, and we started shoveling the neighbors' driveway. At first the kids were griping and complaining about missing their favorite television show, but by the time we neared the end of the driveway, they had gotten into the spirit of the task and were working cheerfully. That night, when I tucked them into their beds in their separate rooms, they each talked about how good it felt to help someone else. Their souls, and mine, were nourished by the lessons learned that day.

APPLY: *How can you nourish your own soul by being kind? Do something kind for someone this week, without being asked and without drawing attention to yourself. Notice how it feels to help someone else.*

Rewards for Real Loving

Peter answered him, "We have left everything to follow you! What then will there be for us?"
Jesus said to them, "I tell you the truth. . . . Everyone who has left houses or
brothers or sisters or father or mother or children or fields for my sake,
will receive a hundred times as much and will inherit eternal life."

MATTHEW 19:27-29

Real loving is not easy. It will cost you more than you can imagine, but it will reward you more than you ever dreamed.

When Peter wondered if all his sacrifices were worth it, look at how Jesus reassured him.

If you give yourself to God and to others, God will register your sacrifice in heaven's ledger sheets. He will pour out a return so bountiful that, over a period of time, you will marvel at how full your life is. You will find yourself breaking out in spontaneous bursts of worship. You will hear yourself singing, "You satisfy my soul. You give me life in all its fullness." Today's imitation love offers no such rewards.

As my professor said, "True personal fulfillment never comes through self-gratification." Instead, it comes through sacrifice. Those sacrifices are real, but so are the rewards that God brings when you make them.

PRAY: *Spend some time thanking God for his promises of blessing and ultimate reward for living a life of real love.*

MONDAY *A Pattern for Prayer*

*If my people, who are called by my name, will humble themselves and pray
and seek my face and turn from their wicked ways,
then I will hear from heaven and will forgive their sin and will heal their land.*

2 CHRONICLES 7:14

Developing prayer fitness is like developing physical fitness: we need a pattern to avoid becoming imbalanced. Without a routine, we will probably fall into the "Please God" trap: "Please God, give me. Please God, help me. Please God, arrange this." Oh, occasionally we'll toss a few thanks heavenward when God allows some good thing to come our way. Every once in a while, if we get caught with our hand in the cookie jar, we'll confess a momentary lapse of sound judgment. And now and then, if we're feeling really spiritual, we might even throw a little worship into our prayers—but only as the Spirit leads.

If I sound sarcastic, it's because I'm a real pro at imbalanced prayer and can tell you from personal experience where it leads. Sensing the carelessness and one-sidedness of our prayers, we begin to feel guilty about praying. And when praying makes us feel guilty, pretty soon we stop praying.

If that has happened to you, a prayer routine can strengthen your faith and improve your spiritual balance.

APPLY: *Do you have a prayer routine? Commit to learning more about prayer and setting up a prayer routine.*

Adoration: Entering Holy Space

I will extol the LORD at all times; his praise will always be on my lips.
Glorify the LORD with me; let us exalt his name together.

PSALM 34:1, 3

It is absolutely essential to begin times of prayer with adoration, or worship. Adoration sets the tone for the entire prayer. It reminds us whom we are addressing, whose presence we have entered, whose attention we have gained. How often our problems and trials and needs seem so pressing that we reduce prayer to a wish list! But when we commit ourselves to beginning all our prayers with adoration, we have to slow down and focus our attention on God.

Walking into some churches, we are gripped for a moment. We say to ourselves, "This is holy ground. I need to concentrate, to focus on what's going on here." Our initial pause adds meaning to the service that follows. Likewise, when we begin our prayers with adoration, we set the tone for our meeting with God. It puts our problems in perspective, and delights the heart of our heavenly Father.

PRAY: *Using the psalm above, spend some time adoring God. If you have trouble, simply use the psalmist's words and make them your own.*

> Ascribe to the LORD, O mighty ones,
> ascribe to the LORD glory and strength.
> Ascribe to the LORD the glory due his name;
> worship the LORD in the splendor of his holiness.

PSALM 29:1-2

Adoration reminds us of God's identity and inclination. As we list his attributes, lifting up his character and personality, we reinforce our understanding of who he is. Often I begin my prayers by saying, "I worship you for your omnipotence." When I say that, I'm reminded that God is able to help me, no matter how difficult my problem seems to me. I also worship him for his omniscience. No mystery confounds God; he will not have to scratch his head about anything I say. I worship God for his omnipresence. Wherever I'm praying—in an airplane, in my car or on some remote island—I know he is present with me.

We can praise God for being faithful, righteous, just, merciful, gracious, willing to provide, attentive, unchanging. When in a spirit of adoration we begin going through God's attributes, we soon say from the heart, "I am praying to a tremendous God!" And that motivates us to continue praying.

JOURNAL: *Take the psalm above, or another one, and paraphrase it. Write it in your own words, as an act of worship, and also as a way to more fully understand what it is saying.*

 *Children of God*

> *How great is the love the Father has lavished on us,*
> *that we should be called children of God! And that is what we are! . . .*
> *Everyone who has this hope in him purifies himself, just as he is pure.*

1 J O H N 3 : 1 , 3

Adoration purifies the one who is praying. When we have spent a few minutes praising God for who he is, our spirit is softened and our agenda changes. Those burning issues we were dying to bring to God's attention may seem less crucial. Our sense of desperation subsides as we focus on God's greatness, and we can truly say, "I am enjoying you, God; it is well with my soul." Adoration purges our spirit and prepares us to listen to God.

God is worthy of adoration. It should be hard to get past the "Our Father" in our prayer without falling back in awe at that incredible miracle. A God who is omnipotent, omniscient and omnipresent and yet who loves us, watches over us, gives us good gifts—this is amazing! Our heavenly Father is worthy of our worship, and so at the beginning of our time with him, let's offer him praise.

P R A Y : *Spend some time adoring God, not to get anything from him, but simply because he is worthy of it. Notice how focusing on God's greatness puts your own demands into proper perspective.*

How to Adore God

His mercy extends to those who fear him. . . . He has performed mighty deeds with his arm;
he has scattered those who are proud. . . .
He has brought down rulers from their thrones but has lifted up the humble.
He has filled the hungry with good things.

LUKE 1 : 50 - 53

How do we adore God? What better way than to list his attributes? Sometimes I think of every attribute I can. Other times I focus on one I have been especially aware of in recent days. When facing major decisions, I may concentrate on his guidance. When suffering from a feeling of inadequacy or guilt, I may praise him for his mercy. When in need, I may worship him for his providence or power.

Adoration is foreign to most Americans, and you will probably feel clumsy when you first do it. As with anything else you take up—racquetball, computer programming or a new job—you have to get disciplined, stretch yourself and work at it to do it well. After a while you progress in both comfort and proficiency. Adoration becomes a way to connect deeply with the God who loves you.

A P P L Y : *Pick out a psalm of praise and read (or sing) it to God. Some of the best known are Psalms 8, 19, 23, 46, 95, 100 and 148; the Magnificat (Luke 1:46-55); and Zechariah's song (Luke 1:68-79).*

The Discipline of Adoration

Praise the LORD.
How good it is to sing praises to our God,
how pleasant and fitting to praise him!

PSALM 147:1

When is it appropriate to adore God? When should we praise him? According to the Bible, we should always give him adoration. He is worthy of our praise.

But sometimes, it's not easy to get ourselves into a worshipful frame of mind. We don't feel like it. We're having a bad day, or we think God hasn't given us what we want. And if we don't feel anything, to praise him would be insincere, right? Authentic worship should flow out of our feelings toward God, right?

Well, not always. Sometimes, we need the discipline of prayers of adoration to bring us into the presence of God. The mark of a courageous faith is one that does not depend solely on fickle feelings. In fact, our feelings flow out of our thoughts, and we can, by thinking about God's attributes, change our feelings. Praying prayers of adoration can lift our spirits, but our motives should be obedience, not a desire for some spiritual "high."

APPLY: *An old worship song says, "Think about his love. Think about his goodness." When we start there, thinking about God's goodness, we will be moved to give him what he deserves: praise and adoration.*

MONDAY

Confession: Naming Our Faults

When a man or woman wrongs another in any way and so is unfaithful to the LORD,
that person is guilty and must confess the sin he has committed.

NUMBERS 5:6-7

Confession is probably the most neglected area in personal prayer today. We often hear people pray publicly, "Lord, forgive us for our many sins." A lot of us carry that approach into our private prayer. We throw all our sins onto a pile without so much as looking at them, and we say, "God, please cover the whole dirty heap."

This approach to confession, unfortunately, is a colossal cop-out. When I lump all my sins together and confess them en masse, it's not too painful or embarrassing.

I determined that in my prayers, I would deal with sin specifically. For example, instead of admitting I had been less than the best husband, I would say, "Today I willfully determined to be self-centered, uncaring and insensitive. It was a calculated decision. I walked through the door thinking, *I'm not going to serve her tonight. I had a hard day, and I deserve to have things my way.* I need your forgiveness for the sin of selfishness." It takes courage to be that honest, but honest prayers can help us really grow.

PRAY: *What specific sins have you committed recently? Review your day; ask God to show you where you have made mistakes.*

Confession's Benefits

> *As far as the east is from the west,*
> *so far has he removed our transgressions from us.*

PSALM 103:12

When you have the courage to call your sins by their true names, your conscience will be cleansed. *I finally said it,* you will think. *I'm finally getting honest with God. I'm not playing games anymore, and it feels good.* You'll begin to learn the meaning of peace, and will feel free to pray, "Please give me your strength to forsake that sin from here on out."

Many Christians don't take confession seriously enough. If we did, our lives would be radically different. When you're totally honest about your sins, something happens. About the fifth day in a row that you have to call yourself a liar, a greedy person, a manipulator or whatever, you say to yourself, *I'm tired of admitting that. With God's power, I've got to root it out of my life.*

As God goes to work on your sins, you begin to see Paul's words being fulfilled in your life: "If anyone is in Christ, he is a new creation; the old has gone, the new has come!" (2 Corinthians 5:17).

JOURNAL: *Write your specific confessions in your journal each day for a week. At the end of the week, look for patterns. Write a prayer asking God to make you a new person.*

Pulling Down the Barrier

"Come now, let us reason together," says the LORD.
"Though your sins are like scarlet, they shall be as white as snow;
though they are red as crimson, they shall be like wool."

ISAIAH 1:18

The amazing thing is that God himself wants to pull down the barrier that has come between us. The Scriptures tell us that the God we have sinned against, the God we have shaken our fist at, holds out his arms to us and says, "Come on back. You don't want to live that kind of life, do you? You don't want to go where that path leads. Admit your sin. Tell me you're fouled up. Agree with me that you're on the wrong track. Come on back, and we'll relate closely again. Once again your prayers will be rich and real. We'll walk together again."

The good news is that you can come back into fellowship with the Father right now. You can say a prayer of repentance. When you pray that prayer, God will restore you. You'll pray a different kind of prayer after that. With God's loving help, you'll be back on track again.

PRAY: *If you want to be restored to God, pray like this: "God, I'm sorry for _____. Please forgive me. I want to turn from this, and I want to come back into relationship with you."*

My Own Worst Problem

When I kept silent, my bones wasted away through my groaning all day long. . . .
Then I acknowledged my sin to you and did not cover up my iniquity. . . .
And you forgave the guilt of my sin.

PSALM 32:3, 5

Imagine returning from a vacation to discover that the person you hired to mow your lawn didn't do so. Fortunately your neighbor has often offered the use of his John Deere mower, which will cut anything. On the way to his house, your neighbor's little dachshund waddles up and starts bothering your pant legs. Now, you hate this dog. It howls, it messes on your lawn, and it snaps at you—which is exactly what it's doing right now. Exasperated, you give the little fellow a sly, swift kick. Then you look up and see your neighbor, arms folded, looking straight at you. Is it a good moment to ask for the lawn mower? Or is there something you need to clear up first?

God offers us free access to all his resources. But some of us have a few things we need to clear up before taking him up on his offer. Thankfully, he's always willing to listen.

PRAY: *Is there some unacknowledged sin in your life? Confess it to the Lord. Then you will be forgiven and in a good place to ask for God's favors.*

F R I D A Y   *Give Thanks*

> *Praise the LORD, O my soul, and forget not all his benefits.*
>
> P S A L M   1 0 3 : 2
>
> *Give thanks in all circumstances, for this is God's will for you in Christ Jesus.*
>
> 1   T H E S S A L O N I A N S   5 : 1 8

As you receive God's forgiveness and marvel at his mercy, confession will naturally lead to the next step in your prayer routine—thanksgiving.

Parents, you know how it feels when one of your children spontaneously thanks you for something. One summer I took my son Todd to the county fair, and as we started back home, my tired little boy fell asleep. A few minutes down the highway, though, he had his arms around my shoulders. "Dad, I want to thank you for taking me to that fair," he said. His words moved me so much, I felt like turning the car around and going back for round two! God is our Father, and he too is moved when we express our thanksgiving.

I thank God every day for four kinds of blessings: answered prayers, spiritual blessings, relational blessings and material blessings. Almost everything in my life fits into one of those categories. By the time I've gone through each category, I'm ready to go back to adoration for all God has done for me. What an awesome God we serve!

PRAY: *What do you feel grateful for? Express your thanks to God. Be specific about all the things he's done for you.*

One Thankful Leper

Ten men who had leprosy met [Jesus].
They stood at a distance and called out in a loud voice, "Jesus, Master, have pity on us!"
When he saw them, he said, "Go, show yourselves to the priests."
And as they went, they were cleansed.
One of them, when he saw he was healed, came back, praising God in a loud voice.
He threw himself at Jesus' feet and thanked him—and he was a Samaritan.

LUKE 17:12-16

As you read the story of the ten lepers, what do you think? How many of those men do you think felt tremendous gratitude as they walked away from Jesus, completely healed of their incurable, disgusting, socially isolating disease? There's no question about it—all ten did. But how many came back, threw themselves at Jesus' feet and thanked him? Just one.

In this story we catch a glimpse of Jesus' emotions. He is moved: first to disappointment by people who felt gratitude but didn't take the time to express it, then to satisfaction by the one who came all the way back to say thanks. When I remember that my expressions of gratitude can evoke that kind of response in Jesus as well, I'm motivated to take time to say thank you to him.

APPLY: *Do you distinguish between feeling grateful and expressing thanks? Watch for moments to be grateful for; then thank God for his blessings.*

MONDAY

Make Requests

> *In everything, by prayer and petition, with thanksgiving,*
> *present your requests to God.*
>
> PHILIPPIANS 4:6

As you pray, it's right to focus on God first. But then it's time for supplications—requests. If you have adored him, confessed your sins and thanked him for all his good gifts, you're ready to tell him what you need.

Nothing is too big for God to handle or too small for him to be interested in. Still, I sometimes wonder if my requests are legitimate. So I'm honest with God. I say, "Lord, I don't know if I have the right to ask for this. I don't know how I should pray about it. But I lift it to you, and if you'll tell me how to pray, I'll pray your way." God honors that kind of prayer.

PRAY: *Is there something you need but have not asked God for? Spend some time praying in this routine you have learned: Adoration, Confession, Thanksgiving, Supplication (ACTS). Ask God to show you what to pray for.*

Getting Specific

Which of you, if his son asks for bread, will give him a stone? . . .
If you, then, though you are evil, know how to give good gifts to your children,
how much more will your Father in heaven give good gifts to those who ask him!

MATTHEW 7:9, 11

Praying specifically leads to tangible, measurable answers—results that strengthen our faith.

One way to pray specifically is to break your requests down into categories: ministry, people, family and personal. Under *ministry*, I pray for the church staff, the construction programs, the public services and all the subministries of our church. Under *people*, I pray for Christian brothers and sisters in leadership positions, the elders, the board, the sick, my non-Christian friends. Under *family*, I pray for my marriage and children. I ask God to make me a godly husband. I ask him for help with decisions about finances, education, vacation time. Under *personal*, I pray about my character. I say, "God, I want to be more righteous. Whatever you have to bring into my life to transform my character, bring it on. I want to be conformed to the image of Christ."

JOURNAL: *Break up your requests into categories, and then keep a list of what you've prayed about. After about three weeks, go back and reread your list. You may be amazed at what God has already done.*

Getting Motivated

> *Until now you have not asked for anything in my name.*
> *Ask and you will receive, and your joy will be complete.*

JOHN 16:24

Do you ever find it hard to find time to pray? For me, the greatest prayer motivator is answered prayer.

When I pray about a sermon and God answers by giving me an insight from his Word or a way of organizing the material, I'm motivated to pray about the next sermon I work on.

When I pray for someone who doesn't know the Lord and one day the person calls me up and says, "I've given my life to Christ," I'm motivated to continue praying for the other seeking people on my list.

When I pray over a difficult decision and then get a sense of God's leading, follow his leading and see by hindsight that I made the best possible choice, I'm motivated to pray about all the decisions that come my way.

And when I pray about a need that cannot be met by any human means and God meets it through his miracle-working power, I'm motivated to get down on my knees and pray for all kinds of needs.

JOURNAL: *Make a record of some of the things you are praying about so that you can look back and see how God answers prayer.*

Turn Over Your Concerns

Cast all your anxiety on him because he cares for you.

1 PETER 5:7

Once I've worshiped God, confessed my sins and given thanks, it's okay for me to take out my shopping list. I used to be vague about what I needed. "Please help me and cover me and keep me out of trouble." I don't do that anymore. I list specific requests, leave them with God and regularly review them to see how he has answered them.

When I get up from praying, I feel as if a ton of bricks has been lifted off my shoulders. When I pray, I'm not just telling God my problems. I'm turning my biggest concerns over to him. Once I've put them in his capable hands, I can go about my day in his strength, free from crushing concerns.

JOURNAL: *Write down your most pressing concerns, being as specific as possible. Keep track of how God answers your prayers. Once they are written down, imagine them being in God's care, so that you no longer have to worry about them.*

Is God Deaf?

Jesus told . . . them that they should always pray and not give up. . . .
"Will not God bring about justice for his chosen ones,
who cry out to him day and night?"

LUKE 18:1, 7

You're discouraged. You prayed fervently that your dad would survive the surgery—but he didn't. You prayed that your son and daughter-in-law would stay married—but they wouldn't. You prayed that your business would withstand a new competition—but it couldn't.

You know that your sins are confessed and your requests are not selfish. And now that your dad has died, your kids are divorced or your business is defunct, it's too late for God to be telling you "wait."

Apparently prayer just doesn't work. Why waste your breath? If heaven doesn't listen, if God doesn't care, or if God lacks the power to change things, why pray? If you've ever had a crushing disappointment that prayer did not fix, you've probably asked yourself these questions.

I do not have a pat answer for you. But I can tell you what Jesus said: Keep on praying. The Father does listen. He cares deeply about everything that affects us. True, he doesn't answer every prayer the way we fallible humans wish he would. But he loves us.

APPLY: *What can you do to build a courageous faith that does not lose heart, even when it seems prayers are unheard?*

"I Kept On Praying"

The Lord is not slow in keeping his promise, as some understand slowness.
He is patient with you, not wanting anyone to perish, but everyone to come to repentance.

2 PETER 3:9

Some years ago we had a baptism Sunday where many people publicly affirmed their decision to follow Christ. I thought my heart would explode for joy. Afterward, in the stairwell, I bumped into a woman who was crying. I couldn't understand how anyone could weep after such a celebration, so I stopped and asked her if she was all right.

"No," she said, "I'm struggling. My mother was baptized today."

This is a problem? I thought.

"I prayed for her every day for twenty years," the woman said, and then she started crying again.

"You're going to have to help me understand this," I said.

"I'm crying," the woman replied, "because I came so close—so close—to giving up on her. But I guess I just kept praying, even though my faith was weak. I kept praying, and she gave her life to Christ, and she was baptized today."

The woman paused and looked me in the eye. "I will never doubt the power of prayer again," she said.

PRAY: *Do you feel tempted to give up on a request you've prayed for a long time? Pray right now for that concern, and for the strength to endure in your prayers.*

MONDAY

Rich Toward God

> *A certain rich man produced a good crop. . . .*
> *[He said to himself] "You have plenty of good things laid up for many years.*
> *Take life easy; eat, drink and be merry."*
> *But God said to him, "You fool! This very night your life will be demanded from you." . . .*
> *This is how it will be with anyone who stores up things for himself*
> *but is not rich toward God.*

LUKE 12:16-21

I like that phrase: *rich toward God.* What does it mean to be rich toward God? I think it means to give God what he desires most, which is a relationship with us. Some of us give ourselves lavishly and freely—richly!—to all sorts of people, activities, achievements and responsibilities. We devote our time, energy, creativity and attention to our education, work, friends, families and pleasures. But we forget about God. We never consider what it means to be rich toward him.

In Jesus' parable, the man's barn full of grain was useless in the end. He had invested his prime time and energy in storing up mountains of riches, but he had invested nothing in what mattered the most, and he stood before God empty-handed.

APPLY: *How much of your time and energy do you invest in what matters most? least? Have the courage to choose the things that will make you rich toward God.*

Don't Forfeit Your Soul

What good is it for a man to gain the whole world, yet forfeit his soul?
Or what can a man give in exchange for his soul?

MARK 8:36-37

You can't trade riches for your soul. What about you? Have you been pouring all your time and energy into building bigger barns while neglecting your relationship with God? Take the initiative to become rich toward God. Whether you're at the beginning of your spiritual journey or stopped at a roadblock along the way, decide now to determine your next necessary step. Do you need to be more disciplined in personal reflection and prayer, in studying the Bible and other Christian literature, in fellowship with Christians and in regular church attendance? Determine your next step, and then take it. Commit yourself to spiritual initiative. You'll receive a payoff that will last for all eternity.

PRAY: *If you are not sure what your next step is, pray for God's guidance. Ask other wise and mature Christians to pray for you and with you. As you begin to sense what your next step is, ask God for the strength to follow through and take that step.*

Teach Your Children Values

Do you see a man skilled in his work? He will serve before kings.

P R O V E R B S   2 2 : 2 9

She sets about her work vigorously; her arms are strong for her tasks. She sees that her trading is profitable, and her lamp does not go out at night.

P R O V E R B S   3 1 : 1 7 - 1 8

It is an honorable goal to help your children financially; I look forward to helping my children financially as they pursue their educations, establish their careers, and marry and start families (if God so leads them). But parents must not allow such help to foster irresponsibility in their children.

When my daughter, Shauna, was eleven, she got a part-time summer job in a beachwear shop owned by a friend of mine. At thirteen, my son, Todd, got a job washing boats at a small-town marina. I wanted both my kids to learn at an early age what it feels like to work hard, to meet the standards of a boss, to earn money, to pay for items they need or want and to enjoy a satisfying sense of independence. I believe that such experiences will serve them well throughout their lives.

P R A Y : *If you are a parent, ask God to help you guide your children toward financial responsibility. If not, talk to God about the lessons you learned growing up. Thank him for the things your parents taught you, or ask for his help if you need it.*

Better Broke Than Bound

The borrower is servant to the lender.

PROVERBS 22:7

For several years after starting Willow Creek Community Church, I received no salary because the church had no money beyond what was needed to rent facilities for our services. My wife, Lynne, taught private flute lessons, and I moonlighted for my father's wholesale produce company. We were so strapped financially that we had to take in boarders and sell personal possessions. Even then we were dependent on the occasional bag of groceries left anonymously on our front porch.

One day a bank sent me an unsolicited credit card. My first thought was, *My ship has come in! Now I can buy some furniture. Now I can buy some clothes. Enough of this constant scarcity.* There was only one problem: Lynne and I would not have the money to pay off the credit card at the end of the month. So there I was, holding a credit card in my hand, while God was saying to me through this little proverb, "Do you know what's worse than being broke? Being in bondage. Don't compound the pain of financial scarcity by enslaving yourself to debt."

I cut up the credit card and threw it away. That was a step toward freedom.

APPLY: *Are you in debt? What steps could you take (seeing a financial advisor, cutting up your credit cards, establishing a budget) to begin setting yourself free?*

Wisdom of Giving

> *Honor the LORD with your wealth,*
> *with the firstfruits of all your crops [your income];*
> *then your barns will be filled to overflowing,*
> *and your vats will brim over with new wine.*

PROVERBS 3:9-10

I remember reading this passage in those early days of our church. It seemed like a long shot to me, but what did we have to lose? We were barely making it anyway: our income in 1975 was about eighty dollars per week. I remember asking Lynne to get the checkbook out and write another tithe check for eight dollars. No matter what, we were going to follow the path of wisdom.

I look back at that time and thank God for his wisdom. I realize how seriously the wrong decisions could have affected our family. It was some time before our barns were overflowing—our children often wore hand-me-down clothes, and for years our only vacations were those provided by gracious friends—but we never lived with the burden of indebtedness, and in time we were blessed to be able to give to others from our abundance and to offer more to God's work than the tithe. As a family we have good reason to be committed to the wisdom of Proverbs.

PRAY: *Do you tithe? Do you believe God's promise to bless your life if you give to his work? If not, ask God to help you increase your trust.*

Whoever can be trusted with very little can also be trusted with much.

LUKE 16:10

Some people with limited resources figure there's too little to worry about. They get lazy, thinking, what difference will it make if they let a few dollars fritter through their fingers here and there? Even the most responsible stewardship wouldn't transform their tiny pile of cash into anything worth paying attention to, so why bother?

Let me say it as kindly as I can: That's twisted thinking. The only way to enhance the capabilities of limited resources is through meticulous stewardship and aggressive initiative. Can we justify carelessness because the numbers are small? On the contrary. Be faithful with little, says Jesus, and someday you will have opportunity to prove your faithfulness with greater things. I don't know whether the "much" of Jesus' statement indicates an increase in financial resources, an increase of some other kind of responsibility in the kingdom or an increase in growth and faith. I suspect it means all three, but what does it matter? Jesus calls us to be faithful in little, and promises a reward that he deems worthy. What greater incentive do we need?

A P P L Y : *Have you been careless with your little? Have you taken it lightly and frittered it away? How can you honor God with the little bit that you have?*

MONDAY *Careful with Wealth*

Command those who are rich in this present world not to . . .
put their hope in wealth, which is so uncertain, but to put their hope in God,
who richly provides us with everything for our enjoyment.
Command them to do good, to be rich in good deeds, and to be generous and willing to share.

1 TIMOTHY 6:17-18

Sometimes folks with excess aren't careful money managers. They never have to sweat a missed payment or an unmet material need, so why worry about it?

How we handle money matters. It matters to God, who sees it as one indicator of our obedience to Christ. It matters to our children, who learn from our example. It matters to the poor, whose state of well-being may hinge on our generosity. It matters to the church, whose God-honoring purposes will be either thwarted or facilitated by the giving of God's people. We cannot afford to be lazy when it comes to money matters. There is too much at stake.

Wealth is a gift from God, not to be hoarded, not to be trusted as security, but to be freely enjoyed and generously shared and used as a tool for multiplied good deeds. Handle it accordingly.

PRAY: *Have you been careless with your much? Have you used it selfishly and withheld a potential blessing to others? Respond to the Spirit's prompting. God will bless you.*

Good Works

> *For we are God's workmanship, created in Christ Jesus to do good works,*
> *which God prepared in advance for us to do.*

EPHESIANS 2:10

On Saturday mornings, many Willow Creek attendees meet in the church parking lot and drive downtown to work with some of our church's inner-city ministry partners. Often when I come to church late on Saturday afternoons to prepare for our evening service, I run into people just returning from the city. They're usually standing around in little groups saying, "Man, I've never worked so hard in my life—and I've never felt so good!"

Why do we feel good when we do good? The main reason is that we are made in the image of a God who is by nature good. That means that he, and therefore we, has enormous capacity for doing good, and we naturally delight in doing good. Each time we live up to that goodness potential, God himself smiles and says, "Ah, that's exactly what I hoped you would do." We sense that smile and those words as an inner affirmation of who we are and what we have done.

We were created to do good works. When we do them, we fulfill our purpose for being alive.

JOURNAL: *Write about a time you served others. Did it give you a sense of purpose? Did it deepen your connection with God?*

Helping Others

The laborer's appetite works for him; his hunger drives him on.

PROVERBS 16:26

This verse provides a guide for our acts of kindness. Personal needs or desires can sometimes motivate us to work diligently and provide for ourselves. Consequently, any acts of goodness that diminish the recipients' drive to work hard and meet their own needs is misspent goodness. It undermines development of people as responsible human beings and creates in them an unhealthy dependence on others.

As a board member for an international Christian relief organization, I have frequently been part of the difficult discussions surrounding relief care and charity. The organization I serve exists to help those who truly deserve and need intervention; to that end, it distributes hundreds of planeloads of food each year to impoverished or tragedy-struck regions around the world.

But what do we do when local farmers decide that rather than plowing their fields and planting seeds and harvesting crops, they'll wait for the planes to show up? We can't afford to make mistakes in this regard. If necessary intervention crosses a fine line and creates an unhealthy dependence, a well-intentioned airlift of supplies could undermine an entire local economy. It takes courageous faith and discernment to walk this line.

APPLY: *How could you help someone in need in such a way that you would not create an unhealthy dependence? Pray for wisdom, and then step forward to help.*

Those Who Deserve It

Do not withhold good from those who deserve it, when it is in your power to act.

PROVERBS 3:27

Being finite human beings, we have limited resources of time and energy; we can't respond to every need in the universe. Committing random acts of kindness may be a nice idea and a catchy slogan for mugs and bumper stickers, but in reality we may have to apply a bit of thoughtful strategy to our doing of good deeds.

When the wise writer of this proverb tells us to do good to those who deserve it, he implies that there are some people who may not deserve it. Some poor people legitimately need help, and we are called to help them. There is no doubt about that calling. But the Bible also teaches in the clearest terms that those who try to take advantage of goodness don't deserve it. God tells us not to waste our limited supply of goodness on conniving people who are trying to avoid taking personal responsibility for their lives. There is more to living out the image of God than indiscriminately performing good deeds.

APPLY: *It's easy to focus on the people we think don't deserve our help. But who is someone who could use your help? Take a specific action this week to help that person. If you're not sure how to help, call and ask what they need.*

Setting Boundaries

> *A Samaritan . . . [brought the wounded man] to an inn and took care of him.*
> *The next day he took out two silver coins and gave them to the innkeeper.*
> *"Look after him," he said, "and when I return,*
> *I will reimburse you for any extra expense you may have."*

LUKE 10:33-35

The Samaritan did a great deal for the wounded man; he literally soiled his hands with the blood of the man's wounds, and he virtually wrote a blank check to cover the man's care. But this famous parable is not a call to indiscriminate goodness.

There are some important things the Samaritan didn't do. While he did take the man to an inn, he didn't cancel his trip in order to care for him. Perhaps it was a business trip, and his boss was counting on him. Or maybe the trip was a family responsibility that he rightly deemed a higher priority. At any rate, he continued on his journey.

We can assume that the Samaritan returned and paid the man's tab, as he had promised to do, but Scripture makes no indication that he continued his relationship with the man in any way. It is okay to set boundaries on our good works.

PRAY: *Read the entire Good Samaritan story in Luke 10:25-37, and ask God to show you if you need to be more compassionate, or work on setting more boundaries.*

Spiritual Sniff Tests

Do not give dogs what is sacred; do not throw your pearls to pigs.
If you do, they may trample them under their feet, and then turn and tear you to pieces.

MATTHEW 7:6

We must ask tough questions of anyone to whom we are considering giving our time or money. Does this organization do exactly what it claims to do? Good intentions and impressive goals are not enough. Are the goals being reached efficiently, effectively and honorably? Does the organization or ministry exhibit fiscal responsibility? Are fundraising percentages reasonable? Are salaries justified?

We also need to apply what I call The Holy Spirit Sniff Test. When we bring a particular form of ministry or good deed before God in prayer, do we sense that God affirms both the particular ministry and our involvement with it? If we do, then the Bible would say to us, "Don't hold back! Shower the place with your goodness. Bless, serve, pray, give, volunteer as much as you can. Let the goodness flow like a mighty river." But if we have any reservations, we mustn't be naive. Our resources of time, energy and money are limited; we mustn't throw them away on unworthy causes or ineffective endeavors. When we give to others, we must be discerning.

PRAY: *Has someone asked for your help? Ask God for discernment about whether to become involved, and strength to do what he says.*

MONDAY

Good Deeds Left Undone

Is this not the kind of fasting I have chosen:
to loose the chains of injustice and untie the cords of the yoke,
to set the oppressed free and break every yoke? Is it not to share your food with the
hungry and to provide the poor wanderer with shelter?

ISAIAH 58:6-7

Every time I fail to do an act of goodness that is in my power to do, I fumble an important ball. And that particular ball is never thrown again. If I don't obey God's promptings to help someone, I miss an opportunity to let God nourish my soul. If I don't help someone, will someone else? Maybe. Maybe not.

It may well be that the vast majority of unmet needs that bring sadness, heartache, loneliness and despair into human lives are merely the flip sides of good deeds left undone. Think about that. Think about the incredible power of good deeds; think about the tragedy of our failure to do them. When it comes to good deeds, God and others are counting on us. If it is in our power to do good, we had better do it.

APPLY: *What good deeds have you left undone? When it is in your power to do good, do you do it? What steps could you take to work with God to remove obstacles so that you can nourish your soul by helping others?*

Working with Our Lavish God

If you spend yourselves in behalf of the hungry and satisfy the needs of the oppressed,
then your light will rise in the darkness. . . .
The LORD will guide you always; he will satisfy your needs.

ISAIAH 58:10-11

We need to remind ourselves every day that we are made in the image of a God who is lavish in doing goodness, a God who delights in redeeming, restoring, refreshing, rebuilding and revitalizing, a God who has called us to do the same. Imagine how our world would be transformed if the approximately two billion people in the world who call themselves Christians were doing the goodness they have the power to do. Imagine what would happen if they were allowing God to do his work of loving and healing and uplifting through them. Now imagine living in a world where all six or seven billion people were doing that.

Why don't we live in a world like that? Because the world is full of people like you and me who don't let the call to goodness penetrate our hearts and minds and souls and mouths and hands and feet. If we want to build a courageous faith, we must heed and obey God's call to help others.

PRAY: *Ask God to give you a clear vision of the difference you could make in the world. Listen for his direction; then obey his leadings.*

Never Enough?

> *Martha was distracted by all the preparations that had to be made. . . .*
> *"Martha, Martha," the Lord answered, "you are worried and upset about many things,*
> *but only one thing is needed."*

LUKE 10:40-42

Many good-hearted people live with a "never-enough" cloud hanging over their heads. Though they willingly pour themselves out in acts of goodness for others, they never sense the smile of God or experience the nourishment of their own souls, because thirty seconds after completing one good deed they start beating themselves up for not doing more. They are unable to unhook themselves from the needs they see around them, and they have slid into a spiral of despair. They have become so consumed with the sadness of our sin-stained world that they have lost touch with the simple joys of being alive.

To these people the Bible says, "The family of God is a huge family with many people to share the responsibility for doing good. When it is in your power to do good, do it. When it is not, then breathe a genuine prayer of concern and intercession, and ask God to provide someone else to meet that need."

APPLY: *Do you ever beat yourself up for not doing "enough" for God? Do you sometimes lose touch with the joyful side of life? Explore the reasons why you might feel that way.*

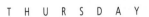

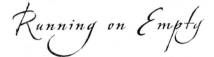
Running on Empty

> *But even if I am being poured out like a drink offering*
> *on the sacrifice and service coming from your faith, I am glad and rejoice with all of you.*
> *So you too should be glad and rejoice with me.*

PHILIPPIANS 2:17-18

Sacrificial love has just one problem. If you really commit yourself to it, you will quickly find out that it is extremely exhausting. After a certain amount of giving and serving and expending, you may begin to feel numb, as if you have nothing left to give. You are running on empty.

It is possible to run completely out of love and then refill the tank. It is possible to love people not only sacrificially but also steadfastly. This is what God calls us to do—not to run the hundred-yard dash in loving people, but to run the marathon. In order to do that, we have to learn how to refuel ourselves when we run out of love. Often, we need God's help to refuel, and he's glad to offer it.

JOURNAL: *List words that describe how you are currently feeling about giving and serving. Be as honest as you can; don't try to edit yourself. Based on this list, would you say your tank is full, quickly running out or totally dry?*

God Replenishes Us

When David and his men came to Ziklag,
they found it destroyed by fire and their wives and sons and daughters taken captive.
So David and his men wept aloud until they had no strength left. . . .
David was greatly distressed because the men were talking of stoning him. . . .
But David found strength in the LORD his God.

1   S A M U E L   3 0 : 3 - 6

David has been loving and leading and helping and serving people until he is nearly out of love. His tank is almost dry when an opposition force ambushes the camp and carries off the wives and children of David and his men. The men, outraged, talk of overthrowing David and even killing him. David can't take any more. He feels like pitching his leadership position. He would like to spit on the ground and leave the people. He's sick of them, and he's exhausted. What can he do?

The answer is found in verse 6: "David encouraged himself in the LORD his God" (KJV). He left the people with their incessant demands. He turned his back on still more opportunities for service. He took time out, got away by himself and had a long talk with God until his spiritual energy supply was replenished.

APPLY: *When you are feeling overwhelmed or exhausted, do you find your strength in the Lord? What would happen if you took time for solitude with God?*

Get Off the Treadmill

Crowds of people came to hear him and to be healed of their sicknesses.
But Jesus often withdrew to lonely places and prayed.

LUKE 5:15-16

Like David, Jesus also took time for solitude after long periods of loving, serving, healing, counseling and teaching. He needed time alone with the Father to replenish himself. It goes without saying that if David and Jesus needed spiritual refueling from time to time, so do we.

Somehow we must learn to slow down, get off the treadmill, seek out solitude and encourage ourselves in God. One way to do this is through a daily time of solitude, perhaps before the events of the day rush in. Talk with the Lord and read his Word. Allow him to regenerate your spiritual energies. Some people find spiritual refueling by listening to Christian music. Sometimes when I'm driving to an appointment, feeling stretched to the limit, I turn off the news with its catastrophes and commercials and put in a worship CD. After a half-hour on the road, my spirit is refreshed by the Spirit of the Lord. Even the strongest faith is bolstered by time alone with God.

PRAY: *Take some time today to be still and be alone with God. Pray about the pressures you are facing, decisions you must make. Read the Bible and reflect on what it means in your life.*

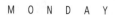

M O N D A Y *Emotional Refueling*

> *Above all else, guard your heart, for it is the wellspring of life.*
>
> PROVERBS 4:23

It is important to watch your spiritual fuel gauge, but you also have to watch your emotional fuel gauge as well. It is possible to keep your spiritual reserves replenished and still feel all out of love.

Major life changes can drain you emotionally: the death of a spouse, divorce, personal injury or illness, loss of employment, change of residence. Even happy events, such as family holidays or the birth of a child, can leave you emotionally spent.

A friend of mine recently had five extremely difficult conversations in one workday. When he left the office that evening, he was doing great spiritually—but he was emotionally depleted.

Emotional depletion also happens at home. The sink backs up and the plumber is busy until the end of the week. Chicken pox attacks the children one by one. You learn that your teenage son has a drug problem. When your emotional tank is empty, you are likely to feel uninterested in the well-being of others, no matter how full your spiritual tank is. Take time to fill your emotional tank!

JOURNAL: *Draw a fuel gauge in your journal, with a needle indicating how full you feel your emotional tank is today. What changes or stresses have affected your emotional reserves?*

TUESDAY *God~Appointed Rest*

There are six days when you may work, but the seventh day is a Sabbath of rest,
a day of sacred assembly. You are not to do any work;
wherever you live, it is a Sabbath to the LORD.

LEVITICUS 23:3

How do you replenish yourself emotionally? First, relaxation. Some people cannot accept that. They prefer to get emotional refueling from a pill or an injection. But there is no quick solution. To fill up your emotional reserves, you need to wind down, take a break, put your feet up, take deep breaths and hold the phone calls.

The second way to replenish yourself emotionally is recreation. Some activities seem to inspire you, to re-create your enthusiasm for life. For my wife, it's reading, writing and playing the flute. For me, it's sailing. For you, it may be walking the dog, playing racquetball or weeding the garden. You may have to experiment for a while to find what works best for you. When you find it, you'll know. A couple of hours of the activity, whatever it is, will refuel you emotionally and make it possible for you to go back to loving others sacrificially and steadfastly.

APPLY: *Why did God give us the command of a Sabbath? What would your emotional tank look like if you took a day each week to rest, worship God and enjoy recreation?*

WEDNESDAY *Get Some Rest*

The angel of the LORD . . . said, "Get up and eat, for the journey is too much for you."
So [Elijah] got up and ate and drank.
Strengthened by that food, he traveled forty days and forty nights.

1 KINGS 19:7-8

One Wednesday before Thanksgiving, I attended a lengthy meeting before driving with my family to Michigan. Although we did not get to bed until five in the morning, we had to get up early and start visiting with relatives. Spiritually and emotionally, I was in fine shape that morning. But physically I was shot.

Every conversation was like hard labor. Someone would tell a joke and I would think, *Don't be a jerk, Bill—laugh!* Relatives came to me hoping for input on a major decision they were making, and a little voice in my head was saying, *I didn't come here to do counseling. I came for turkey and football. If you want an appointment, call my secretary.* I tried hard to hide how I really felt, but not until after I had time to recuperate physically did I feel like myself again.

Physical exhaustion keeps us from following God fully. That's why rest is so necessary, not just for our bodies, but for our souls.

JOURNAL: *Write about a time you were worn out physically. How did it affect your relationships? your ability to pray?*

Fuel for the Race

Do you not know that your body is a temple of the Holy Spirit,
who is in you, whom you have received from God?
You are not your own; you were bought at a price.
Therefore honor God with your body.

1 CORINTHIANS 6:19-20

How is it that we manage to separate the issue of how we treat our bodies from our devotion to Christ? Not just our spirits but also our bodies have been claimed and redeemed and loved. In some mystical and incomprehensible way, the Holy Spirit indwells our bodies and thereby calls us to use our bodies to honor his presence.

When I raced motorcycles, if I wanted to compete well in a race I had to get the finest racing fuel I could find. Anything less than that would inhibit the performance of the cycle. The same is true for us. Our bodies are God's greatest creation, but we can't expect their highest possible performance unless we use the highest-quality fuel.

Honoring God with our bodies means paying attention to where we go, who we let touch us, how we take care of ourselves. It means we keep our bodies away from sin, protect them from abuse and actively pursue physical health. That takes courage, but it's essential.

PRAY: *Ask God to show you where you are failing to honor him with your body. Ask him for the courage to change.*

FRIDAY *Caring for God's Temple*

Don't you know that you yourselves are God's temple
and that God's Spirit lives in you?
If anyone destroys God's temple, God will destroy him;
for God's temple is sacred, and you are that temple.

1 CORINTHIANS 3:16-17

How do you stay physically fit? You know the three rules. Eat right, sleep enough and exercise. Most Americans eat too much sugar and fat; consequently, many of us are overweight, suffer from sugar highs and sugar lows, or even have heart disease. Many of us are careless about sleep. If you do not wake up reasonably refreshed, maybe you are not spending enough time in bed. Or maybe your sleep is inhibited by the coffee you drank all day. And for far too many of us, our major form of exercise is walking down the hall to the photocopy machine. We say we don't have time or energy to exercise, yet experts have medically proven that exercise replenishes our energy.

If you are spiritually and emotionally on track, but still feel burned out, check your diet, your sleep and your exercise. A few simple changes might be just what you need to refuel your tank and refit you for steadfast, sacrificial loving.

APPLY: *How could you change your daily routine to take better care of your body?*
How much easier would it be to be loving if you got more sleep every night?

Care for Your Body

"Everything is permissible for me"—but not everything is beneficial.
"Everything is permissible for me"—but I will not be mastered by anything.
"Food for the stomach and the stomach for food"—but God will destroy them both.
The body is not meant for sexual immorality, but for the Lord, and the Lord for the body.

1 CORINTHIANS 6:12-13

What is the Spirit saying to you about your body? What are you saying back? Few challenges in life are met with as many excuses as our responsibility for caring for our bodies.

Our bodies are so alive with conflicting desires, so attuned to pleasures and pains, so tempted by immediate gratification. Responding in a God-honoring way to these natural drives and desires requires more discipline and determination than almost anything else. It also requires a conscious submission to God's purpose for our lives, which is to be a pure dwelling place for his own Spirit. It's not easy, but whatever progress we make toward honoring God with our bodies will bring direct benefit into our lives. Our self-esteem will increase, along with our physical and mental energy, and our relationship with God will be enhanced. It's a win-win-win deal.

JOURNAL: *Which of your physical appetites tempt you? Write about one or two habits that you could begin to reflect your desire to honor God.*

M O N D A Y

Sharing His Glory

> *And we, who with unveiled faces all reflect the Lord's glory,*
> *are being transformed into his likeness with ever-increasing glory,*
> *which comes from the Lord, who is the Spirit.*

2 CORINTHIANS 3:18

Paul writes that those whom God chooses for his family members he makes "conformed to the image of his Son" (Romans 8:29 NRSV)—he gives them character qualities like those of their elder brother, Jesus.

He does this through the work of the Holy Spirit, his representative in our hearts. The Spirit writes Jesus' own character traits on our hearts: "love, joy, peace, patience, kindness, goodness, faithfulness, gentleness and self-control" (Galatians 5:22-23).

After adopting us and making us like Christ, God invites us to claim our inheritance—the same glorious reward claimed by the triumphant Jesus after his resurrection. Jesus is eager to share his inheritance with us. He will not take the spotlight alone. Instead, "when Christ, who is your life appears, then you also will appear with him in glory" (Colossians 3:4). When Jesus Christ reveals himself in glory to the whole world, he will bring us—his brothers and sisters—with him to share his glory eternally.

APPLY: *The promises of Scripture are not just for someday in heaven. We are, even now, being transformed. We are, even now, exhibiting the fruit of the Spirit. Is this true of your life? Why or why not?*

TUESDAY *Needed: Character*

> *If anyone would come after me,*
> *he must deny himself and take up his cross and follow me.*

MATTHEW 16:24

What does it take to do the will of the Father? It takes *courage* to join a family that is misunderstood by the world. It takes *discipline* to accomplish the tasks God has set out for his children. It takes *vision* to overcome inevitable problems and to see what God is doing in the lives of his children. It takes *endurance* to stick with your brothers and sisters when it would be so much easier to go your own way. Above all, it takes *love* to hold God's family together and to reach out and invite others to join it—tender, tough, sacrificial, radical love.

In a word, it takes *character* to do God's will—and, wonder of wonders, Christ's character is what God offers us when we timidly say we would like to be part of his family. He wants to help us to obey him. If we're willing, he gives us the power to do his will.

JOURNAL: *Write the italicized words from the entry above in your journal:* courage, discipline, vision, endurance, love, character. *How are you doing in these areas? Are you more courageous or less than you were a year ago? Write about the growth you see in your own life in these areas.*

Questions for God

Search me, O God, and know my heart;

test me and know my anxious thoughts.

See if there is any offensive way in me, and lead me in the way everlasting.

PSALM 139:23-24

I have several questions I regularly ask God:

- What's the next step in developing my character?
- What's the next step in my family—with Lynne and the kids?
- What's the next step in my ministry?

Depending on your situation, you might ask:

- What's the next step in my vocation?
- What direction should my dating relationship go?
- How should I plan my giving?

Whatever you ask the Lord, you will be amazed at the way he leads. Once you are quiet and tender before him, waiting to hear him speak, he will bring a verse to mind or will guide your thoughts and feelings. As you build the discipline of stillness into your life, you will find these quiet moments in God's presence becoming incredibly precious to you.

P R A Y : *Spend some time asking God one or two of the questions discussed above. Then spend time listening for his answers.*

If any of you lacks wisdom, he should ask God,
who gives generously to all without finding fault, and it will be given to him.

JAMES 1:5

Sometimes, I don't know how to pray. But I find that God will help me in this regard. He'll give me wisdom. When I feel uncertain about my motives or requests, I say, "God, this is my heart on the matter, and I'd really like you to do this. But if you have other plans, far be it from me to get in the way. You've asked me to make my requests known, and that's what I'm doing. But if what I'm asking for isn't a good gift, if the time isn't right, if I'm not ready to receive it, no problem. Your ways are higher than my ways, and your thoughts higher than my thoughts. If you have different plans, we'll go your way." It takes courage to submit to God, but he blesses us when we do.

APPLY: *How willing are you to pray a prayer like the one above? Are you willing to go God's way, even when it seems different from what you want?*

This Is It

> *Blessed is the man who does not walk in the counsel of the wicked*
> *or stand in the way of sinners or sit in the seat of mockers.*

PSALM 1 : 1

This life that you and I are living today is real life. This is not the teaser before the movie. This is not the pregame show. This is it. The Bible says the adventure of life was designed to be experienced in community.

Don't think that if you wait long enough three close friends will show up on your porch, ring your doorbell and say, "Here we are. Let's do the rest of life together." It doesn't work that way. We each need to take initiative. If we want to make life work, we need to put together a personal development team. If we want to become all God has in mind for us to be, we need to surround ourselves with godly people who can challenge and encourage us, who can share life's joys and sorrows with us. If we only have one chance at life, why not do it the way God designed it? Why not link arms with some brothers and sisters and walk closely with them?

JOURNAL: *If you have a group of friends you walk closely with, write about the influence and blessings you've received from them. If not, write three steps you will take to form such a group.*

Pursuing God's Program

I urge you to live a life worthy of the calling you have received. . . .
[The Spirit] gave some to be apostles, some to be prophets, some to be evangelists,
and some to be pastors and teachers, to prepare God's people for works of service,
so that the body of Christ may be built up.

EPHESIANS 4:1, 11-12

When I was in my twenties, an older Christian man asked me what I was going to do with my life that would last forever. He said, "Bill, I see lots of fire in you for making money and creating an exciting lifestyle. But what about spiritual things? What about God's program for transforming people and changing the world? You're willing to put your best efforts into pursuing your program. But what about God's program?"

His words brought me face to face with the most fundamental questions a person can ask: What am I going to do with my one and only life? What am I going to do that will touch people? What am I going to do that will make a difference eternally? Those questions haunted me and ultimately opened my eyes to God's calling on my life. Perhaps you should ask those same questions.

APPLY: *What are you going to do with your one and only life? Courageously step out in faith "so that the body of Christ may be built up."*

Material in this devotional is
adapted from the following books:

Finding God in the Storms of Life © 2002 by Bill Hybels

Making Life Work © 1998 by Bill Hybels

Too Busy Not to Pray © 1988, 1998 by Bill Hybels

Who You Are When No One's Looking © 1987 by Bill Hybels